THE LIFE OF AUGUSTINE

THE AUGUSTINIAN SERIES

VOLUME 1

The Life
of
Saint Augustine

by

Possidius
Bishop of Calama

Introduction and Notes
by
Cardinal Michele Pellegrino

edited by
John E. Rotelle, O.S A.

AUGUSTINIAN PRESS
1988

Nihil Obstat: James McGrath
          Censor Librorum
Imprimatur: Anthony J. Bevilacqua
          Archbishop of Philadelphia

The introduction and notes were translated into English by
Audrey Fellowes; the biography and notes were translated
by Matthew O'Connell.

The introduction with its notes and the notes to the
biography were taken from *Vita di S. Agostino,* Edizioni
Paoline, 1955. The English translation of the biography was
based on the Latin critical text as prepared by Cardinal
Pellegrino.

Library of Congress Catalog Card Number: 88-71357
ISBN: 0-941491-19-6
          0-941491-09-9 (series)

AUGUSTINIAN PRESS
P.O. Box 476
Villanova, PA 19085

Contents

Part I
The Life and Activity of Augustine
A Chronological Account
(Chapters 1-18)

Part II
Augustine's Everyday Life
(Chapters 19-27, 5)

Part III
Last Years and Death
(Chapter 27, 6 — 31)

Foreword

A Trail of Many Centuries

Siena, Crakow, Goa, Acolman, Mombasa. What have they in common? These and many other places in Europe, Asia, America, and Africa are linked by the thread of Augustinian Tradition, a tradition whose roots reach back to Saint Augustine and North Africa in the fourth and fifth centuries, and whose historical record began in Italy in the year 1256 when the Order of Saint Augustine came into being. This thread of tradition has been picked up from time to time in unexpected places by various observers. Graham Greene, for example, in chapter three of his *Another Mexico*, speaks of a visit to Acolman, the imposing sixteenth century monastery built by Augustinian friars from Spain near the pyramids of Teotihuacán, north of Mexico City. Recalling his impressions of the size, the beauty, and the wonder of the place, he writes:

> In the cloisters are the remains of the oldest wall paintings in Mexico — the faint line still visible of some representation of Hell and Judgment whitewashed over when that lesson had been learned by the Indians, the crude and elementary idea of punishment in terms of flame and cauldron and pincers. What remains today is the last and most difficult lesson of all — the lesson of love and the mysterious death of the Creator on the cross, and the little quiet European countryside, copied by Indians, still going quietly and securely on as the Universe ends: with both a sun and a moon in the sky.

The *Augustinian Series* proposes to be a kind of historical searchlight, scanning the centuries of the Augustinian tradition. By drawing the readers' attention here and there throughout the centuries, the series will examine and illumine various places and persons, especially writers and other notables — such as saints and blessed — who are the living components of the tradition — living, that is, in the sense that their influence continues to be felt today in a particular way by those women and men who are the followers of Saint Augustine and who shape their lives in accord with his *Rule*. Others too will be enriched, we trust, by this series which will contain a variety of writings, some of them original compositions and others selected translations. Each volume in the series will illumine some portion of the common thread that runs along a trail of many centuries. The series will begin, fittingly, with a life of Augustine by Possidius, his close friend and companion, who offers us the earliest biography of the giant figure in whose shadow the trail began.

Arthur J. Ennis, O.S.A.

Introduction

AUTHOR

THE SOURCES OF OUR KNOWLEDGE of Possidius[1] are to be found in the *Life of Saint Augustine* by Possidius, the letters of Augustine, Prosper's Chronicle, and a few official documents referring to the African churches. Possidius lived in close and harmonious friendship with Augustine for about forty years (31, 11). This is a good deal longer than the time he spent in Augustine's community, and so he must mean that the cordial relations between them continued even after he was obliged to leave the monastery on his nomination as bishop.

It is from Possidius himself that we learn that after Augustine was ordained priest at Hippo, no doubt inspired by the example set by Ambrose, and in continuation of the kind of life he had already entered on at Thagaste, here too he was not long in founding a monastery close to the church, in a garden given to him by Bishop Valerius. Its members lived together, renouncing the right to dispose of their own property (5, 1; see Augustine's Sermon 355, 1-2). Now since Augustine began exercising the functions of his priesthood at Easter 391, three years after his return to Africa (3, 1-2),[2] and died in 430, the forty-year friendship with Possidius must have dated from the very beginnings of the monastery at Hippo. And since Augustine died at the age of 76, and our author outlived him by at least seven years, he may well have been somewhat younger than Augustine.[3]

From his fairly detailed account of Augustine's ordination as priest (5) he seems not to have been present at it,[4] from which we may conjecture he was not a native of Hippo.

In the community which he founded Augustine was the acknowledged master, from whom Possidius, like the rest of his companions, received the Lord's bread,[5] that is, the salutary teachings of the divine word as expounded by Augustine.

Possidius himself has given us a picture of the kind of life that was lived in this house. Taking the life led by the holy apostles as a model (5, 1), they prayed, fasted, applied themselves to good works, and meditated on the law of the Lord (3, 2). All personal possessions were strictly forbidden, and each received food and clothing (25, 1) according to his need (5, 1). This was distributed by a cleric whom Augustine assigned by roster to the office of steward, and who was obliged to give him an account of his management at the end of the year (24, 1). Furnishings and clothing were simple, but kept in good order (22, 1). Meals were taken together (25, 1) and were frugal, consisting mainly of herbs and vegetables; meat was reserved for guests and the sick; there was always a little wine, in carefully specified quantity (22, 2; 25, 2). Silver spoons were used, and serving dishes were of earthware, wood, or marble (22, 5). They enjoyed reading at meals; but as Augustine was busy all day, preaching (31, 4 and passim), hearing court cases (19, 1-5), taking part in councils and public debates with heretics (14, 1; 17), visiting his diocese (12, 1), helping the needy (27, 1-2), and as meals were practically the only time when the community could gather round its head, conversation also had its share, all the more as guests often appeared (22, 6). So many things were discussed, and it was a feast for these clerics, who regarded Augustine with such great admiration and affection, to listen to him recounting his experiences of the apostolate. Sometimes they themselves were witnesses to the marvelous conquests made by divine grace through his words. An uncharitable insinuation would sometimes threaten to disturb this atmosphere of serenity and concord, but Augustine checked any hint of slander with the utmost severity, even to reproving harshly some of his episcopal colleagues who had offended in this way (22, 7-8; 25, 4-6). There was another point on which he was very particular. There must be no swearing. Whoever broke that rule would see his ration of wine reduced. However, Augustine knew how to be tolerant or intervene as the case required (25, 2-3).

Women, even next of kin, were infrequent visitors to the house. If any had need to come there, Augustine would receive her in the company of several clerics (26). The widespread influence enjoyed by Augustine meant that various churches, even some of the most important, would apply to him when they wanted a bishop. So from time to time one of these clerics would have to leave the community to take charge of a diocese. This happened to a dozen or so of Augustine's disciples, among them also Possidius, after about six years of a happy life in that peaceful oasis.

In 397 occurred the death of Megalius, bishop of Calama, a city of the proconsular province of Numidia situated between Cirta and Hippo,[6] and primate of Numidia.[7] The bishopric must have been vacant for some time, and perhaps there was an immediate successor to Megalius of a bishop whose name has not come down to us, and who at any rate could only have been briefly head of that church which we shall find entrusted to the care of Possidius.[8]

The description he gives us of the daily life of Bishop Augustine, as far as it concerns the habitual occupations of a bishop of the fourth century, is equally true of himself: preaching, court hearings and sentencing, attendance at councils, the perpetual guard against heretics, helping widows, orphans, and the sick, recommendations and interventions with the authorities, training of the clergy, supervision of the management of church and monastery, besides of course constant prayer, made up a program of work more than enough to fill his day.

We may be sure that the new bishop was among those of Augustine's disciples who were anxious about the training of the clergy, and so also encouraged the monastic life in their own church, where clerics were trained in chastity and poverty and prepared to preach the word of God. Perhaps from that monastery too there went out priests and bishops destined to propagate the salutary teaching of the Church (11).

Under the weight of his new responsibilities Possidius would certainly many times have had to resort to the advice of the one whom he still revered as master, even though he had become his colleague. We have a letter addressed to him by Augustine in which he answers certain questions about feminine ornaments and ends with an allusion to the ordination of Donatists.[9] This letter, which the Maurists place in class IV, comprising those of uncertain date, was probably written, acording to Tillemont,[10] in the early years of Possidius' episcopate and after 401, as the question of the ordination of Donatists was dealt with at the council of Carthage on 16 June of that year. If we have no other record of his correspondence with Augustine, it may be due to the fact that the two bishops met fairly often, and so could discuss matters in person.

On 25 August 403 Possidius is present, with Augustine and Alypius, at the eighth council convened at Carthage to give notice of suitable means for winning back the Donatists to the Catholic Church.[11] In accordance with the decision taken by the assembly he had to summon his colleague Crispinus, Donatist bishop of Calama, to attend a conference at which Catholics and Donatists would meet together; he was answered with a refusal disguised by petty arguments. In fact, a few days later (this happened in 404), when Possidius was on a pastoral visit to a country district in his diocese, he was attacked by Donatists who surrounded the house he had taken refuge in with armed men, stoned and set it on fire. Finally breaking down the door they entered the house, wounded and carried off the travelers' horses, and insulted and struck the bishop himself. The Donatist bishop Crispinus, as a heretic, was fined 10 pounds of gold, but after he had denied the charge of heresy a public debate took place between the two bishops of Calama, at the insistence of Augustine who thought this essential for the enlightenment of the people. Three meetings took place there, at the end of which Crispinus was declared a heretic by the proconsul, but Possidius intervened in his favor to obtain the remission of his fine. Crispinus appealed, but the judgment was upheld; even so the Catholic bishops again interceded for the remission of the penalty, which was granted. This episode, which echoed far and wide in the history of the struggle against Donatism, has been narrated to us by Augustine[12] and by Possidius himself (12) who speaks in the third person, suppressing his own name.

We have news again of Possidius in 407, when he was chosen at the eleventh council of Carthage, together with Santippus, primate of Numidia, Augustine, and four other bishops, to hold a public debate with the same number of representatives of the faithful of Germania Nova, to judge the controversy which had arisen between these and their Bishop Maurentius;[13] the outcome of such a move is unknown to us.

The following year the bishop of Calama was again involved in a painful incident, this time with pagans, still evidently in formidable strength in those parts. At Calama on the first of June they celebrated a solemn religious feast, during which the procession of dancers passed before the very doors of the Church. When the churchmen tried to stop the outrage, the pagans answered by stoning the sacred building. Since a law of 24 November 407 prohibited pagan religious feasts, eight days later the bishop turned to the municipal council appealing to the law. The good will shown by the authorities was answered by more stone throwing from the fanatics. The next day the clergy asked for their protest to be recorded, but were not listened to. The bursting of a violent hailstorm that very day on Calama seemed to be heaven's answer to such crimes. For a third time, however, the pagans stoned the church, and then set fire to both the church and the priests' house, killing one of the priests. Possidius himself had great difficulty in reaching a safe hiding place, where, from about four in the afternoon till late at night, he listened to the crowd searching for him and clamoring for his death. Augustine then came to Calama to comfort the Christians and admonish the pagans, who in the meantime had calmed themselves and were in fear of the rigors of the law. There followed an exchange of letters between Nectarius, an influential citizen of Calama, pagan son of a Christian father, and Augustine. Nectarius acknowledges the evil committed by his fellow citizens, and begs for a distinction to be made between innocent and guilty, and that even the latter may be treated with leniency. In his answer Augustine explains how the events had come about, assuring him that the Christians have no thought of vengeance, but that a just and moderate punishment is essential to prevent further excesses and for the good of the guilty themselves.[14]

Toward the end of that year or at the beginning of 409 Possidius left for Italy to seek legal provisions from the imperial authorities, taking with him a letter from Augustine, accompanying Book VI of his *De Musica*,[15] for Memorius, bishop of a city in southern Italy, Capua,[16] according to some. He was glad to take the chance which that journey gave him of visiting Paulinus and his wife Terasia at Nola, to whom he also brought a letter from Augustine;[17] on 27 March Augustine still had no news of the outcome of Possidius' mission.[18]

The following year Possidius again sailed to Italy, as a member of a deputation of four African bishops, which the fifteenth council of Carthage, held on 14 June 410,[19] sent to the emperor to urge the re-enforcement of the laws against pagans and heretics which had been temporarily suspended.[20] Apparently the embassy succeeded, as on 25 August 410 Honorius promulgated a law against heretics and pagans.[21]

An even more notable part was assigned to Possidius at the great conference between Catholics and Donatists held in May-June 411 at Carthage, where the 266 Catholic bishops elected their representatives to speak for all of them — Aurelius of Carthage, Alypius of Thagaste, Augustine of Hippo, Vincentius of Culusi, Fortunatus of Cirta, and Possidius of Calama.[22]

The way in which our author intervened in this debate helps to give us an impression of his mentality, as that of a man who likes positions to be clearly defined and detests all verbosity and quibbling. When Petilian, a Donatist bishop, proclaimed himself and his companions as "bishops of the truth of Christ" (episcopos veritatis Christi Domini nostri),[23] he answers, "one must prove oneself a bishop of the truth, not boast about it" (episcopos veritatis probare opus est non iactare). Then, to Emeritus: "It is written *with much chatter you will not avoid sin* (Proverbs 10:19). As we have an example of this maxim before us, with God's help I hope not to prove myself a wordy speaker. Therefore, if we are all agreed, let us come to a matter which may be treated and resolved quickly, with no need for quibbling and long, drawn-out speeches."[24] And shortly after, when Emeritus had answered: *Hidden wisdom and unseen treasure: of what value is either?* (Sirach 20:29), Possidius insists: "There has never been wisdom in a lot of words."[25]

Later, in support of Augustine's statement: "We are now anxious to bring the principal matter to a close," he adds, "Let no one try insidious ways of delaying us, wanting to know if we have any trust in the defense of our cause."[26] He intervenes yet again to reproach the Donatists for their quibbling and their evasiveness.[27]

In reality, however, it was Augustine who was the Catholics' most effective advocate, and Possidius is right in attributing the principal merit of the victory to him (XIII).

In 412, at the end of a long letter to Volusianus,[28] Augustine sends regards to his correspondent on behalf of "my holy brother and fellow bishop Possidius," who therefore must have been at Hippo at the time, on one of the visits he so gladly made to his master and friend.

After taking part in the provincial council of Numidia held at Milevis in 416, with sixty-one other bishops including Augustine and Alypius Possidius sent a letter, probably drawn up by Augustine, to Pope Innocent, urging him to use his authority and intervene against the dangerous errors of Pelagius and Celestius.[29]

Shortly afterward the name of Possidius appears again, beside those of Aurelius, Alypius, Augustine, and Evodius, in another letter addressed to the same Pope Innocent, where the same errors are explained and confuted in greater detail, proposing that Pelagius, either in person or by letter, should be formally examined and asked to declare his views.[30]

The conference of 411 between Catholics and Donatists, already mentioned, had a sequel seven years later, when Augustine, who had gone to Caesarea in Mauritania with other bishops at the command of the apostolic see, had an encounter there with the Donatist bishop Emeritus, whom he invited to a public debate. In the account which Augustine himself wrote of it,[31] Possidius also figures among the Catholic bishops present, but in Possidius' own reference to the event (14) he mentions only Augustine.[32]

In May 419 Possidius took part in the council of 217 bishops which gathered at Carthage around the legates of Pope Zosimus, who in the meantime had been succeeded by Boniface. This was to settle the case of a priest named Apiarius who after his excommunication by Urbanus, bishop of Sicca Veneria and once a disciple of Augustine at Hippo, had appealed to Rome — a case which had reopened the delicate question of appeals to the apostolic see. With Augustine and Alypius, Possidius was one of the twenty-two bishops appointed by the council, before it disbanded, to remain at Carthage and, with Bishop Aurelius, to settle matters still pending.[33]

The last and fleeting allusion to Possidius which we find in Augustine's writings occurs in Book 22 of *The City of God*, written in 426, where we are told that Possidius had taken to Calama a relic of the martyr Saint Stephen, which twice healed the priest Eucarius.[34]

In 428 Calama too experienced the horrors of invasion by the Vandals and other barbarians, Alans and Goths — devastation, fire and slaughter, and countless other atrocious disasters. Three episcopal cities alone were left standing: Carthage, Hippo, and Cirta. When Possidius saw his city now empty of inhabitants — for we may presume that he acted as Augustine had advised Honoratus, bishop of Tiabe, in Letter 228 which Possidius quotes (30) — with other bishops of the surrounding districts he took refuge at Hippo, where he remained throughout the siege which began in May or June 430.[35] Thus Augustine's disciple and dearest friend had the comfort of being at his side during the last troubled period of Augustine's life. He witnessed the sorrow endured by the Saint, the more profound as his insight into those terrifying and disastrous events deepened (28). Possidius attended him in his last illness, impressed at the sight of his continuous prayer and flowing tears; he was present at his death, and at the celebration of the sacrifice on the day of his burial (29; 31).

The siege lasted till July 431, when the barbarians withdrew. Then Hippo, abandoned by its population, was set on fire (28, 10). We do not know if Possidius had already returned to his see of Calama; at least he certainly returned there after the convention of 1 February 435, which "abandoned by the Vandals the three Mauretanias and part of Numidia, including the city of Calama."[36] But when in 437 Genseric wanted to impose Arianism on his dominions, Possidius and other bishops resisted all the pressures and were driven from their sees.[37] This is the last news we have of him.[38]

It is in these last years that the composition of the *Life* must be placed, that is, between the ending of the siege of Hippo (July, 431), which Possidius tells us lasted fourteen months (28, 12), and the taking of Carthage by Genseric, 19 October 439,[39] which at the time that Possidius was writing was still unharmed (28, 10). The date of composition can probably be narrowed down again to between the death in 432 of Boniface, to whom Possidius seems to refer in the phrase "a certain count Boniface" (28, 12), and the dispersion of the Catholic bishops, exiled as we have said in 437. If Possidius had written any later, in his account of the disasters which befell the African churches in those years he would no doubt have included this.[40]

STRUCTURE

In his preface the author gives some hint as to the method he intends to follow. His aim is to write "about the life and conduct" of Augustine (see also 27, 4), showing what he had seen in him and heard from his lips, beginning at the point that Augustine himself had reached in the *Confessions*, in other words his return to Africa after his conversion. For the preceding period Possidius gives us sufficient information in a brief first chapter.

The twofold subject could be treated in two ways: either by inserting into a chronological narrative of the "life" notes on "conduct," as is usually done in the hagiography of today, or by following the chronological account of events and actions in the hero's life with an exposition of his "conduct," independent of any particular period.

Possidius chose this second way, except that he was careful to postpone his account of the last events of Augustine's life and death till after the description of his virtues. An expedient which was probably suggested by the example of Suetonius,[41] or anyhow by a tradition of which the Roman historian was among the best known representatives, it was also followed by Paulinus of Nola and to a certain extent by Sulpicius Severus, being an undoubtedly useful means of holding the reader's attention in suspense, and constructing a literary work more compact and co-ordinated than it would have been if the writer had first narrated all the events in the hero's life, and then dwelt on his virtues as if by way of an appendix.

The plan of the work thus took shape naturally, in answer to the requirements just mentioned, the subject matter falling into three parts: 1) the life, or chronological account of the events and actions of Augustine's career (1-18, 2); 2) the conduct, taken in a general sense, as an exposition of the hero's public and private conduct in everyday life (19-27, 5); 3) the final events, sickness and death (27, 6-31).

In fact, a phrase in the preface (section 3) would lead us to expect a threefold division somewhat different from the one used in the biography, into a) excursus (birth), b) procursus (career), c) debitus finis (destined end). But as the division which we proposed just before, and which was also indicated by Possidius at the beginning of his preface, though somewhat briefly, is one that presents a more definite character, is clearly realized in the drafting of the work and has its precedents in biographical tradition, we think it is the better one to follow. The formula just quoted, which is taken straight from *The City of God* (see commentary), signifies rather material which the subject itself requires the biographer to deal with, and which may be dealt with in various ways.[42]

In each of these parts the principle which has suggested the order of the subject matter is easily visible. In the first part, as the biographer had not intended to repeat anything which Augustine had spoken of in the *Confessions* (preface 5), he takes few words to run through events prior to the conversion, hardly mentioning the traditional themes of native land, family, and education (mention of which may be suggested by the natural requirements of the narrative, without necessarily inferring the influence of the school),[43] or his first steps in the ascetic life (1-2). There follows a brief account of the life led by Augustine as a layman in the community of friends which formed around him, regarding both his personal exercise of the virtues and the activity of the apostolate in the spoken and written word, an activity which is illustrated by a single episode (3). We are told how he was ordained priest (4) and of his activities in this position; his establishment of a monastery near the church at Hippo; his preaching ministry (5), and his first struggles against the heretics (6-7).

Chapter 8 provides an important turning point, where Augustine's election to the episcopate is described, after which there is a return to the development of the prevailing theme in the presentation of Augustine's activity: the struggle against heresies. This is therefore first of all set out in two periods: that of Augustine's priesthood and that of his episcopate.[44] One episode alone is recorded from the first period, the public debate with the Manichean Fortunatus (6), this being followed by a general account of the heretical movements current at the time in Africa: Donatists and Manicheans, though pagans, are included among them (7, 1; see 18, 7). As for the second period, the biographer divides his exposition into four sections, each devoted to one particular heresy: Donatism (9-14, bearing in mind the wider interests in Chapter 9 already mentioned); Manicheanism (15-16); Arianism (17); Pelagianism (18). This successive treatment again shows the influence of the chronological principle, at least in the place given to the Pelagians, which is clearly justified by Possidius: "against the Pelagians also, a sect new in our times" (18, 1).

Within each of these sections the chronological order, when it is a question of facts that can be dated with certainty, appears to be kept as regards the first, where, speaking of the struggle against the Donatists, Possidius relates the episode of Calama (12), which occurred in 404, then the encounter with Emeritus of 418.

In the third section also, devoted to the Arians (16), there is first an account of the conference between Augustine and Pascentius, which though Possidius gives no chronological indications must have occurred in 406,[45] and then of the public debate with the Arian bishop Maximinus which took place long afterward, probably in 428.[46]

As to the Pelagians (18), a reading of the account is enough to show how the writer keeps to chronological order.

The only exception is to be found in the second section, where the Manicheans are the subject of discussion (16). There Possidius first relates the conversion of Firmus, which occurred before Possidius became a bishop, therefore not later than 400, then the inquiry conducted by Ursus, the palace procurator, which is to be placed in 421,[47] and finally the debate with Felix, held in 404. We can see no convincing reason for such a transposition. Perhaps chronology was not in the writer's mind at this point, and he was content to narrate a sequence of similar episodes of conversion from Manicheanism.

Naturally the principle of relating matters concerned with the various heresies in succession did not allow chronological order to be kept between one section and the other, as may be seen from what we have reported so far. It is not a question here of single events with no connection between them, but of "the aims of life," of continual activity which Possidius, like Suetonius,[48] shows at work not "in time," but "in kind."

Still less could the chronological principle determine the order in the second part, devoted to conduct. Here too we note the influence of the biographical tradition, which treated the public life of the hero first,[49] and then his private life.[50] Chapters 19-21 are taken up with Augustine's public activity, and we hear of his methods in giving judgment (19, 5), interceding with the authorities (19, 6-20), attending councils, and ordaining priests and clerics (21). Then, in treating of Augustine's private life, Possidius describes his clothing, his bed, his meals, the use and administration of the property of the church, the manner of life he expected of his clerics, his behavior with women, and his visiting.

In the third part (27, 6-31) we are told of the spirit in which Augustine awaited death, his last works, especially the *Revisions*, the invasion of the Vandals, cause of so much sorrow to Augustine, his last illness, the letter to Honoratus of Thiabe which Possidius quotes, the last days preceding his death, his death, and the books which he left. In conclusion the biographer invites the reader to thank God with him, and to ask him that he (Possidius) may follow Augustine's example, and one day share in his blessedness.

Here chronological order once more intervenes, as required by the nature of the subject matter. Also in this part importance is given to certain traditionally familiar elements, such as the mentioning of the age at death,[51] the burial, the will, and the inscription on the tomb.[52]

AIM AND STYLE

In what frame of mind did Possidius set about writing the life of Augustine, and how did he intend to present his hero to us? He had been close to Augustine for about forty years, living in pleasant community undisturbed by any disagreement (31, 11; see preface 3); he had seen him fall asleep in the Lord (31, 5); the impression of him he carried in his mind was ineffaceable. To his affection for a friend was added his veneration for a master, a saint, a bishop who had worked, written, and fought so much for the good of the Church. Was it not right that his memory should be handed down to posterity in a biography? This had been done for other men who had arisen through divine grace (preface 3): Paul the Monk, Anthony, Martin, Ambrose. These at least Possidius must have thought of, since he could not have been ignorant of the mention made of them by Paulinus in the preface to his life of Ambrose, written a few years earlier with the encouragement of Augustine, and certainly well known to the community at Hippo.

To write about Augustine was to offer to the Catholic Church an effectively edifying theme, and Possidius' duty as a Christian and as a bishop was precisely to apply himself to such an aim (preface 1). There remained certainly Augustine's writings, evidence of the faith, hope, and love of that bishop dear to God, and source of benefit for the reader (one of such writings, the letter to Honoratus, Possidius inserted into his narrative (30, 2) just because of its usefulness to the priesthood). But even more advantageous was Augustine's personal example for those who had had the luck to hear and see him (31, 9): why not share these benefits with others?

In taking up his pen to write about Augustine, perhaps Possidius had yet another aim in mind, which it was inexpedient to declare openly to avoid seeming to attach too much importance to it: that of defending his memory against accusations and suspicions? Augustine's activity had to a great extent been concerned with the struggle against

Donatists, Manicheans, Arians, and Pelagians, carried on in his writings, in public debates and councils, not without repercussions in the political field. It was natural that in such an inflamed environment even he should be the target of accusations, of which we have evidence in some discourses and polemical writings.[53] Some people even attributed to the *Confessions* the aim of a personal defense, which seems to us excluded by the very nature of the work.

Now one of such accusations is expressly mentioned and refuted by Possidius in the passage where he relates that Augustine ordered sacred vessels to be broken and melted down to provide help for the poor: "I would not mention this if I did not know that it offends the carnal judgment of some people," and he appeals to the teaching of Ambrose (24, 15-16). Elsewhere a probable aim at apology could be pointed out in the passage where we are told of Augustine's reluctance to accept the episcopate while his bishop was still living, a step which he was compelled to take, in ignorance of the prescriptions in force, and which he later disapproved of (8, 3-6; see Augustine, Letter 213, 4).

But since the apologetic note is to be heard only in these passages, it seems logical to think not of a conscious intention from the very beginning to defend Augustine, but rather of a theme which the biographer touched on without previous intention, using a propitious occasion. In any case the apologetic aspect is quite secondary in Possidius' presentation of the "life" and "conduct" of Augustine, and it is precisely in the way he considers and judges his hero that we may perceive the characteristic quality of his writing.

Possidius shows a mentality distinctly clerical common to ancient hagiography. He writes for the edification of the Church and prays the Lord that he may fulfill the expectations of the good children of the Church (preface 1. 4). Possidius has no intention of writing a chapter in the history of the Church. The Augustine he shows us is truly the man he has known, and his personal qualities, his habitual way of life at the center of the small flock of disciples and friends, are what interest his biographer, and he discusses them with complaisance. But he sees all in the light of the mission which providence entrusted to Augustine in the Church, that of priest and bishop.

Already as priest, with his writing and preaching, Augustine comes to the help of the Catholic Church in Africa which at last begins to "lift its head," and the joy at such success is communicated even to the Church overseas (7).

Once he becomes a bishop he makes use of his greater authority to intensify and extend his work for the Lord's Church, which grows and prospers (9, 1). A good number of schismatics, enlightened by his words, return to the peace and unity of the Church, which sees its ranks increase (10, 4-5). His own work for the good of the Church is multiplied by the activity of the bishops and clerics trained in his school who are required by the various churches in Africa and overseas, and by his writings, translated even into Greek (11). The Church's traditions are the norm by which he carefully revises his books (28, 1). As well as in the passages quoted his biographer often likes to note the beneficial influence which Augustine's work has on the growth of the Church (12, 9; 16, 3), and on its peace and unity (13, 1; 18, 5-7).

All his activities are undertaken for the peace and good of the Church (12, 4-5; 14, 7-8), for the edification of the Church's children (18, 9) to keep the faith of the holy Church intact (21, 1). And when, at the end of his account, he states it is plain from Augustine's writings "that that bishop, dear and acceptable to God, lived rightly and entirely in the faith, hope, and love of the Catholic Church" (31, 9), it looks almost as if Possidius intends this as a summing up in rapid synthesis of his hero's whole life and works — in the same way as Augustine himself summarized it, for example, in that phrase which sounds like a plan of action: "We are indeed servants of his Church,"[54] and at the beginning of a letter: "With that care which I am especially obliged to exercise on behalf of the Church entrusted to me, whose needs I serve, and which I desire not so much to be at the head of as to be useful to."[55]

We have to admit that his biographer is right in this judgment. If he shows no understanding of Augustine's greatness as a thinker, which above all must assign him his place in history, he is not mistaken when he sees him as a man of the Church. It has been rightly observed[56] that Augustine's activity as a writer was essentially inspired by pastoral aims and almost always adapted to practical needs.

In his simplicity, then, Possidius has seen more correctly than those moderns[57] who attribute to Augustine attitudes of thought foreign to him, attitudes matured in a time of intellectual crisis when the meaning of traditional Christianity was lost sight of, and try to explain the pretended incompatibility between his understanding of Christianity derived from the gospel and especially from Saint Paul and his adherence to the understanding and practice of the Church.

This insertion of Augustine's work into the life of the Church in no way detracts from the strongly personal character of his religious feeling. On the contrary, it is precisely the intensity of his life as a Christian, in other words his saintliness, which makes an unforgettable man "a leading member of the Lord's body, always solicitous and most vigilant for the good of the universal Church" (18, 6).[58]

Possidius reveals the marks of this saintliness which strike him most, in relating single episodes and later in describing Augustine's habitual ways. Not that in this last part, which we have analyzed above, there is any intention of studying the various virtues of Augustine according to the scheme common to hagiography at that time. The exposition of conduct, meaning precisely the habitual manner of life, gives him a better opportunity to note Augustine's virtues than when he is relating the successive events in his life.

So Augustine is presented as the pastor who does all he can for the good of the Church, in combating heresies, writing, preaching, judging (14; 31, 4, etc.), interceding wisely and discreetly for the accused (20), and attending councils (31), but outward occupations, above all when they lack any obvious religious importance, are a burden to him. His joy is in devotion to prayer and the study of divine matters, and in the fraternal company of those who share his ideals and his daily life (3, 2; 19, 6; 21, 11-12). We think that here Possidius has successfully portrayed the character and inclinations of Augustine, the man we know from his writings he had learned to know from long familiarity with him.

Among Augustine's virtues his biographer stresses the humility, which led him to reveal his faults in the *Confessions* (preface 5-6), and again in his last illness made him shed many tears while assiduously reading the penitential psalms (31, 1-2); the simplicity in his dress, furniture and food, inspired by a sense of moderation, and thus as far from the overrefined as from the slovenly (11, 2; 22, 1-6); the total disinterestedness, even as regards the property of the Church (23, 2; 24); the brotherly love, in his exercise of hospitality, his stern repression of scandalmongering (22, 6-8), his generosity to the poor (23, 1; 24, 15), his constant care for the harmony among his own people (25, 4-6), his concern for widows, orphans, and the sick (27, 1-2); the chastity, which prompted him to a rigorous reserve in his relations with women (26; 27, 3; see 9, 2).

Since it is in divine scripture that the norm of Christian life is to be found, Possidius is careful to show that this was the rule of conduct constantly practiced by Augustine. He followed the Lord's invitation when he renounced all worldly ideals (2, 1-2). Many times Possidius indicates the virtues of his hero with biblical phrases, not only because such a way of expressing himself was natural to one familiar with the sacred books, but it seems obvious — to show how Augustine realized in himself the program for a holy life set out in those books. Augustine meditates on the law of the Lord day and night (3, 2); he lives in a monastery with God's servants in accordance with the rule established in the time of the holy apostles (5, 1); he is the lamp lit and set on the lampstand which gives light to all in the house (5, 5); he is always ready, *as it is written,* to give an account of his faith and hope in God, able to exhort with sound teaching and confute his opponents (6, 3; 9, 1); he follows the teaching of the apostle Paul in his function as judge (19), as also in his use of food and in particular of wine (21, 2-4), and the teaching of the apostle James in visiting the needy (27, 1-2); he follows Mary's example in his love of the spiritual life (24, 12); he wants the words of Jesus to be the norm of relations between brothers (25, 4-6); he is the scribe learned in the kingdom of heaven, the merchant who sells all his possessions to buy the precious pearl, and he puts into practice the Savior's admonition to act and teach (31, 10).[59]

Augustine had admired an exemplary bishop in the figure of Saint Ambrose, who had effectively contributed to his conversion (1, 5-6); his own conduct is inspired by that example (24, 16-17; 27, 4-8).With these remarks Possidius implicitly acknowledges the significance of the Bishop of Milan as a "type" of holiness to which he appeals to justify actions which some people censured in Augustine.

In presenting the saint to us, no disciple of Augustine could fail to give prominence to the work of grace. Augustine is one "predestined" (preface 2); it is God's mercy that inspires Ambrose with the words that enlighten Augustine, it is the divine mercy that little by little sets him free from heresy, divine help which prepares him to receive the doctrine of the Church and the holy sacraments (1, 5-6). In the early days of his new life divine providence works in him (3, 5); by the gift of God Augustine's work raises again a Church oppressed by the Donatists, and a wonderful grace inspires his books and sermons (7, 2-3; 31, 8). God guides his steps on various occasions (14, 3), even saving him by means of men's mistakes (12, 2), and it is the Lord's help which brings an unpleasant incident safely to an end (12, 9). He promotes the peace and unity of the Church with Christ's help (13, 1; 18, 7): and his long life is a gift of God for the benefit of the Church (31, 1).

HISTORICAL VALUE

No one doubts the historical authenticity of the *Life of Augustine*.[60] The protestation of truthfulness which the biographer makes in his preface, in the form of a prayer (preface 4), appears fully credible from what we know of his moral character and his relations with Augustine, as well as from the tone of his writing, and the complete agreement of his narrative with other testimonies, particularly with the works of Augustine himself.

At the very beginning Possidius tells us the principal source of his information: "What I saw of him (that is, Augustine) and heard from him" (preface 1). Many times in the course of the narrative he explicitly refers to events of which he himself and his companions were witnesses (15, 1-6; 22, 8; 24, 5, 17; 28, 13; 29, 1-2; 31, 1-3, 5), or to what he heard recounted by Augustine (4, 1-3 three times; 27, 6, 9).

For certain matters he refers to written documents, especially to the records of the public debates with heretics (6, 7; 24, 7; 16, 2-4; 17, 6-7). He also draws on the works of Augustine, which he mentions at the beginning (preface 5), and on the letters, of which he quotes one in part (20, 3 to Macedonius) and one complete (30, to Honoratus), and mentions the contents of others (8, 5, see notes). Even the letters addressed to Augustine by his correspondents, which were also read by the members of the community,[61] must have been familiar to him, if at least once (8, 2, see note) he expresses himself in the same words.[62]

When he is not sure of some fact he tells us so (15, 5: "If I remember correctly"; 15, 7: "perhaps"). He is rarely content to say he knows something without quoting its source (20, 1; 24, 3; 29, 4).

In studying Possidius' biography from this point of view we naturally wonder if the writer has realized the historical significance of the person he is speaking about. When we think that the person is Augustine, we shall hardly expect from the first narrator of his life a valuation that gives due importance to his gigantic personality. The exceptional greatness of Augustine is for us of an essentially intellectual order; but it is not for everyone to follow the philosopher and theologian to the heights of his speculation; and undoubtedly the very large majority of those who today admire the genius of Augustine owe their opinion to a small few who have approached him with open minds and profound study. On the other hand the distance in time helps us to understand ideas whose fertility we perceive in the development that history has been able to record of them, as only one who contemplates the tree can gauge the power contained in the seed.

Now there is nothing to show us that Possidius was a man endowed with any particular talent for speculation. He was a devout son of the Church, who as cleric and even more as bishop took part in the vicissitudes of the African Church, at that time sorely tried by the various schismatic or heretical movements which we have mentioned many times. Augustine was in the foreground of the struggle against heresy, not because of the post he held, since Hippo was an episcopal see of little importance, but because of the strength of his personality as theologian, pastor, and controversialist. This aspect of Augustine's historical greatness is one which Possidius well recognized. The praise he gives Augustine in regard to it, praise which is no conventional formula but the expression of a deeply rooted admiration, places his hero in a higher sphere. Without repeating what we have already said in showing how Possidius constantly sees Augustine within the framework of ecclesiastical life, it will be enough to quote his biographer's judgment on the outcome of the struggle against Donatism: "And this entire good work (that is, the condemnation of the heretics, the conversion of bishops, clerics, and communities, the peace of the Church) . . . was begun and carried to completion by that holy man, with the approval and cooperation of our fellow bishops" (13, 4).

We must also point out here the profound admiration Possidius had for Augustine's writings, always regarded as means "for the building up of the Church's holy children"

(18, 9). He speaks of Augustine's activity as a writer in the passage just quoted, glancing at his work as a whole accomplished for the benefit of the Church. He returns to the subject in telling us of the revision which Augustine made of his works (28, 1-2), and again at the end, showing the books written by him and those collected in his library as the precious legacy he left to his Church, together with numerous clergy and flourishing monasteries. It is precisely in his writings that he still lives in the midst of the faithful (31, 8-9).[63] Yet despite his enthusiasm, Possidius gives us a balanced and objective portrait of his master, and is not to be drawn into the exaggerations of a Paulinus of Nola, who speaks of the works of Augustine as inspired by God.[64] But the most eloquent proof of the admiration of Possidius for Augustine as a writer is the catalogue of the master's works which he left us, rendering a valuable service to posterity.[65]

In conclusion we should recognize that in presenting Augustine to us as essentially an apostle of Christ's Church Possidius sketched the figure of his hero as he wished him to be, successfully catching one essential aspect of his greatness, even if leaving others in the shadow which history alone would be able to illuminate adequately.

NOTES

Author

1.   Some manuscripts, followed by ancient scholars, confuse the names Possidius and Possidonius; see Papebroch, in Acta S.S. 17 Mai, 4, pages 27f.

2.   Tillemont *Mémoires pour servir à l'histoire ecclésiastique des six premiers siècles,* Venice 1732, Volume 13, page 151.

3.   I see no grounds for the assertion of H. Wright Phillott, DCB, art. Possidius, that Possidius' account shows he was converted from paganism.

4.   Tillemont, *op. cit.,* page 154.

5.   Augustine, Letter 101, 1.

6.   Audollent, art. Calama, DHGE 11 (1939), 334-337.

7.   Augustine, Letter 38, 2.

8.   Tillemont, *op. cit.,* page 299. Morcelli, *Africa Christiana,* Brixen 1816-1817, volume 2, page 326; volume 3, page 422; Weiskotten, page 12; Audollent, DHGE 3 (1924) 335, place the election of Possidius in 397; H. Wright Phillott about 400.

9.   Letter 24, 5.

10.   Tillemont, *op. cit.,* volume 14, pages 256f.

11.   Mansi 3,790; Hefele-Leclercq, *Histoire des Conciles,* Paris 1907, volume I, pages 154f.

12.   Letter 105, 5; Answer to Cresconius, 3, 50-52; see also Tillemont, *op. cit.,* volume 13, pages 398ff.; Morcelli, *op. cit.,* volume 3, pages 20f.

13.   Mansi 3, 806; Morcelli, *op. cit.,* volume 3, p. 34; Hefele Leclercq, *op. cit.,* pages 156-158.

14.   Augustine, Letters 90-91; 103-104; see Tillemont, *op. cit.,* volume 13, pages 463f.; Morcelli, *op. cit.,* volume 3, pages 36f.

15.   Letter 101, 1.

16.   Ughelli, *Italia Sacra,* 6, Venice 1720, page 301; Cappelletti, *Le Chiese d'Italia* 20, Venice 1866, 19f., page 123.

17.   Letter 95, 1. On the date of this letter see P. Courcelle, *Revue des Etudes Ancienne,* 53 (1951), pages 270-276.

18.   Letter 104, 1.

19.   409, according to the *Fasti Consulares,* ed. W. Liebenam pages 41-42; see note Mansi 3, and Weiskotten, *op. cit.,* page 15, number 35.

20.   Cod. Theod. XVI 5, 47; Tillemont, *op. cit.,* volume 13, page 497; Maurini 15, 480; Mansi 3, 810; Hefele-Leclercq, *op. cit.,* volume I, page 159. Weiskotten, *op. cit.,* p. 15, dates the council 1 July, without saying why he rejects the date given in the Records (XVIII Kal. Iulias).

21.   Cod. Theod. XVI 5, 51; Morcelli 3, pages 43f.

22.   Mansi 4, 8ff.; Morcelli, *op. cit.,* volume 3, page 50.

23.   Mansi 4,169C.

24.   Scriptum est: *Ex multiloquio non effugies peccatum* (Proverbs 10:19). Hoc quoniam nos ante oculos habemus, Deo inspirante verbosi videri nolumus. Itaque, si placet, ad causam veniatur, quae proxime agi poterit et definiri, moratorias autem prosecutiones (sic).

25.   *Sapientia abscondita, thesaurus invisus: quae utilitas in utroque?* (Sirach 20:29). "In multiloquio numquam fuit sapientia" (Mansi 4, 172CD).

26.   Principale negotium iam cupimus terminari. . . . Morarum tendiculas nullus interponat, si de causae nostrae defensione aliquam habemus fiduciam (*ibid.* 183C).

27.   *Ibid.,* 211BC.

28.   Letter 137, 20.

29.   Augustine, Letter 176; Morcelli, *op. cit.,* volume 3, page 74; Mansi 4, 335; Hefele-Leclercq, *op. cit.,* volume I page 184.

30.   Augustine, Letter 137; Morcelli, *ibid.*

31.   Answer to Emeritus 1.

32.   Morcelli *ibid.,* page 89.

33.   Tillemont, *op. cit.,* pages 778-782; Morcelli, *op. cit.,* pages 91-97; Hefele-Leclercq *op. cit.,* pages 190f.; Leclercq, *Africa Christiana,* 2, pages 130-134; Duchesne, *Storia* 3, pages 138-143; Audollent, ar. Apiarius, DHGE 3 (1924), 951-954; P. Batiffol, *Le catholicisme de Saint Augustin,* 5th ed., Paris 1929, pages 442-451.

34.   *The City of God* 22, 12.

35.   Tillemont, *op. cit.,* page 940.

36.   F. Lot, Histoire du Moyen-Age, in the Hist. gen. by G. Glotz 1, 1, Paris 1940, page 56; Schmidt. Geschichte der Vandalen, page 62.

37.   Prosp. chron. pages 475, 1327.

38.   Concerning the legendary accounts which tell us that with other bishops he was put on board ship without oars or sails and landed in Puglia, as also concerning the transport of relics to Mirandola where a Saint Possidonius is revered, see Papebroch, Acta S.S. 17 Mai, 4, pages 27ff. The churches of Reggio and Mirandola celebrate his liturgical feast 16 May, the Augustinian Order 17 May.

39.   Audollent, *Carthage romaine,* page 96.

40.   See Harnack, Possidius p. 7.

Structure

41.   See Leo, pages 3-10; Peter, Scriptores Hist. Augustae, page 107ff.

42.   Kemper, pages 38ff., divides the central part into two sections: public life (5 or 6-21) and private life (23-28). We think the proposed division corresponds better to the program which the biographer indicated at the beginning.

43. W. Steidle (pages 127-129) rightly observes that the nature of the subject matter could of itself have led to such a method of composition.

44. The division into four parts proposed by Weiskotten seems to us defective: 1-5, introduction; 6-18, activity against heresies; 19-27, daily life in monastery and church; 28-31, last days and death. In the first part, chapters 1-2 at most can be admitted as introductory, referring as they do to what Augustine has already recounted in the *Confessions* (see preface 5); the second part, though in fact almost entirely concerned with action taken against the heretics, is meant by Possidius to show how much Augustine has done for the good of the Church: that explains chapter 11, which is certainly not a digression or an unimportant addition, since it is devoted to the work of Augustine which illumined the church at Hippo and the rest of the African churches and those "overseas" through the clerics whom he trained and through his books. Besides, we have to remember the distinction made by Possidius between the periods of Augustine's priesthood and episcopate, a distinction clearly marked at the cost of interrupting the account of Augustine's activities against the Manicheans.

Romeis (page 14) also divides the *Life* into four parts: Lebensgang-Taten-Sitten-Lebensende, without further definition; but he fails to understand the distinction our author makes between "life" and "works."

45. See Tillemont, *op. cit.*, pages 438ff., 993, and, for the various facts mentioned in this introduction, our notes to the relative passages.

46. Tillemont, *op. cit.*, page 909.

47. *Ibid.*, page 829.

48. For example, Augustine 9; see Kemper, page 49.

49. For example, Suet. Aug. 61: qualis in imperiis ac magistratibus regendaque per terrarum orbem pace belloque republica fuerit, exposui (I have shown him as military commander and civil magistrate, and regulating state affairs throughout the world in peace and war).

50. *Ibid.*: referam nunc interiorem ac familiarem eius vitam, quibusque moribus atque fortuna domi et inter suos egerit a iuventa usque ad supremum vitae diem (I shall now tell of his private and family life, and of his character and fortune at home and among his own people from youth to the last day of his life). See Kemper, page 46.

51. For example, Tac. Agric. 44.

52. See Leo, *op. cit.*, pages 11-14.

Aim and style

53. For example, *Answer to the Writings of Petilian* III, 19, 30; *Answer to Cresconius* III, 92; IV, 79; *Expositions of the Psalms* 36, sermo 2, 18-20.

54. *The Work of Monks* 37.

55. Letter 134, 1.

56. Altaner, Studierstube, page 406.

57. For example, K. Holl, "Augustins innere Entwicklung," in *Abhandl. d. preuss. Akad. d. Wiss.* 1922, Phil. hist. Kl. 4, Berlin 1923, pages 3-51; reprinted in *Gesamm. Aufsatze zur Kirchengesch* 3, Berlin 1928, pages 54-116, passim.

58. This seems to have been insufficiently appreciated by Harnack, Possidius, passim; see especially page 177.

59. Refer to our notes for the relative biblical passages.

Historical value

60. The vague reservations of Ioannes Clericus (Jean le Clerc) are of no importance; see Salinas, pages VIII-XII.

61. See Letter 27, 2.

62. For allusions to other writings, see the notes.

63. See Romeis, *op. cit.*, page 160.

64. Opus sancti et perfecti in Domino Christo viri fratris nostri Augustini libris quinque confectum, quod ita miramur atque suspicimus, ut dictata divinitus verba credamus (The work composed in five books by our brother Augustine, a man holy and perfect in our Lord Christ, which we so much admire and honor that we believe the words to have been divinely dictated) (Letter 3, 2; see Letter 45, 7; 50, 18).

65. See the critical edition, with full introduction, edited by A. Wilmart, *Miscellanea Agostiniana*, 2, pages 149-233.

BIBLIOGRAPHY

Bonner, Gerald. *St. Augustine of Hippo: Life and Controversies* (Philadelphia, 1963).

Brown, Peter. *Augustine of Hippo: A Biography* (Berkeley and Los Angeles, 1967).

——————————. *Religion and Society in the Age of Saint Augustine* (New York).

Chabannes, Jacques. *St. Augustine*, trans. Julie Kernan (Garden City, N.Y., 1962).

Duchesne, Louis. *Early History of the Christian Church* (3 Vols.; London, 1909-24).

Frend, W. H. C. *The Donatist Church. A Movement of Protest in Roman North Africa* (Oxford, 1952).

Marrou, Henri Irenee. *A History of Education in Antiquity*, trans. George Lamb (New York, 1956).

Meer, F. Van der. *Augustine the Bishop*, trans. B. Battershaw and G. R. Lamb (New York, 1961; paperback ed., with emended trans., in Harper Torchbooks: New York, 1955).

Willis, C. C. *Saint Augustine and the Donatist Controversy* (London, 1950).

PREFACE

The Author's Aim and Precedents for the Work

1 My determination has always been, with the Savior's grace, to serve the almighty and divine Trinity in faith. First as a layman and now as a bishop, I have tried to use whatever talents and literary powers I may have for building up the holy and true Catholic Church of Christ the Lord. I must therefore obey the inspiration of God, maker and ruler of all things, and not keep to myself what I know of the life and conduct of that excellent bishop, Augustine, a man predestined and revealed at the proper time. What I have to say is based on what I saw of him and heard from him.

2 We know from our reading that other devout men belonging to our holy Mother, the Catholic Church, have set themselves a similar task in the past. Inspired by the Holy Spirit, they have used voice or pen to convey, for the information of those desirous of hearing or reading, what they knew of the great and outstanding individuals who lived their human lives in accordance with the Lord's grace that is given to all and who persevered in that grace until death.

3 Therefore, I too, least of the ministers of God, moved by the unfeigned faith (1 Timothy 1:5) with which I ought to serve and please the Lord of lords (1 Timothy 6:15) and all good believers, have undertaken to tell, as well as the Lord allows me, of the origin, progress, and due end of that esteemed man. I shall be handing on what I learned from him and what I experienced myself in many years of close association with him.

4 I pray the supreme Majesty that I may carry out and bring to completion the task I have thus undertaken, in a way that does not offend against the truth that comes from the Father of lights, (James 1:17) or disappoint the loving expectations of the good sons and daughters of the Church.

5   I do not intend to recount everything that blessed Augustine himself has told us in his *Confessions*, where he describes the kind of person he was before receiving grace [in baptism] and the kind of life he lived after receiving it.

6   He wrote as he did in order that, as the Apostle says, others might not believe or think more highly of him than they knew for themselves or had heard about him (2 Corinthians 12:6). With his usual holy humility he refused to practice any deception; he wanted the Lord and not himself to be praised for the deliverance and gifts he had already received, and he relied on the prayers of his brethren for the further gifts he still hoped to receive.

7   Indeed, as the angel authoritatively declared, *it is good to keep hidden the secret of the king, but honorable to reveal and confess the works of the Lord* (Tobit 12:7).

Part I

The Life and Activity of Augustine:
A Chronological Account
(Chapters 1 — 18)

Augustine and Monica listen to the preaching of Ambrose, bishop of Milan, by Jaime Huguet (1415-1492), Catalunya Art Museum, Barcelona, Spain.

CHAPTER 1

Augustine's Life from Birth to Baptism

1   Augustine was born,[1] then, at Thagaste[2] in the province of Africa.[3] His parents were people of good standing and Christians,[4] and belonged to the senatorial class.[5] They brought him up with great care, and went to the expense[6] of an education that concentrated on secular literature; that is, he was steeped in all the disciplines described as "liberal."[7]
2   And in fact he first taught grammar in his home town and then rhetoric at Carthage, the capital of Africa, and later on overseas at Rome and Milan, where the court of Valentinian II resided at that time.
3   The bishop of the latter city in those days was Ambrose, a priest very pleasing to God and outstanding even among the best. This preacher of God's word spoke very often in the church; Augustine was present in the congregation, listening with great interest and attention.[8]
4   At one time, when he was a young man at Carthage, he had been led astray by the errors of the Manicheans.[9] He was therefore more attentive than others to anything that might be said for or against that heresy.   5   And it happened by the mercy of God the Liberator, who touched the heart of his priest,[10] that certain questions regarding God's law were answered in a manner contradicting that error. As a result Augustine was gradually instructed, and little by little that heresy was, by God's mercy, driven from his soul. In a short time he was confirmed in the Catholic faith and conceived so ardent a desire of advancing in religion that he received the divine sacrament at the approaching holy days of Easter.[11]

Notes

1.   On 13 November 354.

2.   Thagaste was a small town that became a free municipality under Septimus Severus. It has been identified with the modern Souk Ahras, which is about 250 kilometers (125 miles) southwest of Carthage and 80 kilometers (40 miles) southeast of Hippo.

3.   Meant is Proconsular Africa, which corresponded to the northern part of Tunisia. This province was not part of the Roman "Diocese" of Africa but was directly under the authority of the emperor.

4.   At the time of Augustine's birth only Monica, his mother, was in fact a Christian. His father, Patricius, did not become a catechumen until Augustine was in his teens (*Confessions* 2, 3, 6; see 1, 11, 17); he received baptism only shortly before his death (*Confessions* 9, 9, 22).

5.   They were *curiales,* that is, members of the municipal *curia* or senate, which represented the town in dealings with the imperial administration.

6.   Augustine speaks in *Confessions* 2, 3, 5, of the efforts his father made to acquire the money for his son's studies in Carthage; later on, Romanianus, a rich fellow townsman, helped Augustine (*Against the Academics* 2, 3).

7.   Possidius is repeating the expression used by Augustine himself (Letter 101, 1, and especially *Confessions* 4, 16, 30); the saint sees an irony in the term "liberal" because while he was studying these disciplines he was himself a "slave" of his passions. In addition to what Possidius says here, Augustine tells us that after his initial studies in Thagaste (*Confessions* 1, 9, 14-15), he studied grammar at Madauros (about 30 kilometers [15 miles] from Thagaste) from the age of twelve or thirteen (*Confessions* 2, 3, 5), and at sixteen went to Carthage (3, 1, 1), where he devoted himself to philosophy and especially to rhetoric.

8.   See Augustine's description in *Confessions* 5, 13, 23.

9.   The Manicheans were named after their founder, Mani (also known to the Latins and Greeks as Manes and Manichaeus), a Persian who lived in the third century A.D. The Manicheans professed a set of gnostic teachings that had for their foundation a belief in two absolute principles: Light and Darkness, Good and Evil, God and Matter. Augustine joined the sect at 19 and remained in it, despite uncertainties and strong doubts, until he was 30.

10.   The meaning is that although Ambrose was not trying to refute the Manicheans, divine providence inspired him with thoughts that would resolve Augustine's doubts; more particularly, they would help him in answering the objections of the Manicheans to the Mosaic Law or, if we take the term "Law" more broadly, in freeing himself from a grossly literal interpretation of the Old Testament; see Augustine, *Christian Instruction* IV, 39.

11.   24 April 387, as Augustine tells us in *Confessions* 9, 6, 14.

CHAPTER 2

He Renounces the World and Gives Himself to God

1 He immediately abandoned with all his heart every worldly ambition. No longer did he seek wife or children, wealth or worldly honors, but resolved, with his companions, to serve God and to be in and of that little flock to which the Lord was speaking when he said: *Fear not, little flock, for it has pleased your Father to give you a kingdom. Sell whatever you have and give alms; make for yourselves purses that do not grow old and a treasure in heaven that will not fail* (Luke 12:32-33), and so on.
2 This holy man also desired to do what the Lord said on another occasion: *If you wish to be perfect, sell all that you have and give to the poor and you will have treasure in heaven, and come, follow me* (Matthew 19:21). His desire was to build on the foundation of faith, not with wood, hay, and straw but with gold, silver, and precious stones.[1]
3 At that time he was over thirty;[2] the only one left to him was his mother, who stayed with him and found far greater joy in his resolve to serve God than in grandchildren.[3] His father was already dead by this time.[4]
4 He also told the students to whom he was teaching rhetoric that they should look for another instructor, since he was resolved to become a servant of God.[5]

Notes

1. See 1 Corinthians 3:12. For Augustine's application of this passage to the ascetical life see *Expositions of the Psalms* 80, 20f.

2. He was thirty-three.

3. Possidius is echoing *Confessions* 8, 12, 30, where Augustine tells of his saintly mother's joy at learning that after her many prayers and tears during the long years when Augustine was astray he was now converted and intending to give himself wholly to God. "The only one" refers to his parents; he still had a brother, Navigius (see *The Happy Life* 6, 14; *Order* I, 5;

Confessions 9, 11, 27 and at least one sister, whom Possidius mentions further on (chapter 26, 1).

4.   Patricius died when Augustine was seventeen and had recently gone to Carthage; see *Confessions* 3, 4, 7.

5.   Augustine's official reason for resigning his chair was a chest ailment that weakened his voice (*Confessions* 9, 2, 13). His resignation came in the autumn of 386, before his baptism. The biographer is not concerned here with exact chronological order but is satisfied to recall the overall event of the conversion and the various incidents attendant upon it.

CHAPTER 3

Monastic Life
and First Manifestations of Apostolic Zeal

1   Having received God's grace through the sacrament, Augustine decided that together with some fellow townsmen and friends who were likewise bent on serving God he would return to Africa and to his own house and property. 2   Thither he went and remained for about three years.[1] He then renounced the property and, with those who had joined him, lived for God in fasting, prayer, and good works and in meditating day and night on the law of the Lord (see Psalm 1:2). The truths which God revealed to his mind in meditation and prayer he communicated to present and absent alike, instructing them in sermons and books.[2] 3   It happened during this period that one of the people known as "imperial agents"[3] was residing in Hippo Regius[4] and learned of his good reputation and teaching. The man was a good God-fearing Christian and had a keen desire to see Augustine, telling himself that if he were only privileged to hear the word of God from his mouth, he would surely be given strength to set aside all worldly lusts and attractions. 4   Augustine learned of this from a reliable person and because he wanted this soul to be delivered from the dangers of the present life and from eternal death, he immediately went of his own accord to Hippo. He met the man, spoke with him often, and exhorted him as persuasively as he could with God's help to fulfill his promises to God.   5   Day after day the man kept promising to do so, but as long as Augustine remained there, he did not carry out his promise. Surely, however, he derived some benefit and fruit from what divine providence was now everywhere accomplishing through this purified and ennobled instrument

(see Romans 9:21) that was ready for the Lord's use in every good work (2 Timothy 3:17).

Notes

1.   From the end of the summer of 386, when he landed in Africa, to the early months of 389, when he was ordained a priest.

2.   To this period belong, in addition to some letters, the works *On Genesis, Against the Manicheans, Music* (in six books which he had begun in Milan), *The Teacher,* and *True Religion.*

3.   *Agentes in rebus* were civil servants whose official duties were to carry imperial messages and supervise the postal service. In practice they served to keep the court informed about the activities of the provincial governors and the military commanders.

4.   Hippo Regius was the city on the Numidian coast, about 2 kilometers (1 mile) southwest of the modern Bona, where Augustine was to serve as priest and bishop. See F. van der Meer (in bibliography), pages 16-20.

CHAPTER 4

Compelled to Become a Priest

1   The bishop of the Catholic Church of Hippo at this time was the saintly Valerius.[1] The needs of the Church required him one day to speak urgently to the people about providing and ordaining a priest for the city. The Catholics already knew of Augustine's way of life and teaching and they seized upon him as he stood peacefully in the congregation, unaware of what was to happen (for, as he used to tell us,[2] when he was a layman he avoided only those churches that needed a bishop).

2   They therefore laid hold of him and, as is customary in these situations,[3] brought him to the bishop to be ordained. With complete unanimity they asked that this be done, and demanded it with fervent cries. Meanwhile Augustine wept copiously; there were some, he himself told us, who attributed these tears to pride and tried to console him by telling him that though he was worthy of better things, priesthood was at least a step toward a bishopric.   3   In fact, however, the man of God, as he told us, was applying a higher standard and was grieving at the many great dangers which the government and administration of the Church would bring upon him; that was the reason for his tears.[4] In the end, however, they had what they wanted.

Notes

1.   "Holy man" or "saint" was an honorary title given to ecclesiastics and especially to bishops.

2.   Augustine tells us this in Sermon 355, 2, which was probably preached at the beginning of 391.

3.   Possidius knew of others who had been ordained against their wishes: for example, Saint Paulinus of Nola, who was ordained a priest at Barcelona by popular demand, as he himself recorded in a letter to

Alypius (Letter 24, 4, among the letters of Augustine); Paulinian, brother of Saint Jerome, who was compelled to accept ordination by Epiphanius (Jerome, Letter 51, 1); Nepotian, of whom Jerome writes in his Letter 60, 10. Possidius tells the same story of Fermus, a Manichean converted by Augustine (see chapter 15, 1). On a similar occasion, Augustine refused to yield to the urging of the populace, who wanted him to ordain Pinianus (Letter 126). On another occasion, a priest whom Augustine had chosen as bishop of Fussala refused the post and could not be ordained (Letter 209, 3).

4.   Augustine expressed these sentiments in a letter to Valerian shortly after his ordination; he asked that he be allowed a period of withdrawal, until the next Easter, so that he might prepare himself for his new mission (Letter 21).

CHAPTER 5

He Founds a Monastery and Begins to Preach

1   Soon after his ordination he founded a monastery near the church and began to live there with the servants of God, following the way of life and rule that had been established under the holy apostles. The most important provision was that no one in that community was to have any property of his own, but rather they were to have all things in common, with each being given what he needed;[1] this was the course Augustine himself had adopted when he had returned home from overseas.

2   Valerius, the holy bishop who had ordained Augustine, was a devout and God-fearing man (see Acts 10:1-2). He rejoiced greatly therefore and thanked the Lord for hearing the prayers which, he tells us, he had so often raised that heaven would grant him a man capable of building the Lord's Church by preaching the word of God and salutary doctrine. Being himself a Greek by birth and insufficiently master of the Latin language and literature,[2] he recognized that he was not up to this work.   3 Contrary to the usual practice of the African Churches, he gave his priest permission to preach the gospel in church even when he himself was present and to hold frequent public discussions. For this reason some bishops were critical of him.[3]   4 This venerable and far-sighted man knew for sure, however, that this was the usual practice in the Eastern Churches. And because he had regard for the good of the Church, he was unconcerned about his detractors, provided only that he saw a priest accomplishing what he knew that he himself, though bishop, could not do.   5 As a result, a lamp lit and burning and raised on a candlestick was now giving light to all who were in the house (see John 5:35; Matthew 5:15).

News of this spread abroad, and, following the good example given, some other priests began with episcopal permission to preach to the people in the presence of their bishops.[4]

Notes

1.   The allusion is to what the Acts of the Apostles has to say about the first Christians, who shared all their goods (Acts 2:44; 4:32-35). Augustine gave an extended and concrete description of his way of life in Sermons 355 and 356. See Van der Meer, 199-206.

2.   Augustine complains about the poor grasp of Latin shown by the clergy of his diocese (Letter 84, 2).

3.   Saint Jerome (Letter 62, 7) likewise deplored this practice. Socrates and Sozomen, Greek historians of the Church, say that it was followed in the Church of Alexandria; they trace it back in this case to the period when Arius, a simple priest, used sermons to spread his heresy. Some distinguished preachers who were simple priests: at Alexandria, Pierius in the third century (Eusebius, *History of the Church* VII, 32, 26-27); at Antioch, Dorotheus, who was heard by Eusebius himself (*History* VII, 32, 204), and later, John Chrysostom; at Nola, Saint Felix (Paulinus of Nola, *Poems* 16, lines 243-244); at Saragossa, Saint Vincent, a martyr, who was an assistant to Bishop Valerius and had a speech impediment.

4.   At Carthage, for example; Augustine and Alypius congratulated Bishop Aurelius for introducing the practice there (Letter 41, 1). In his Sermon 20, 5 Augustine urges the people to listen gladly to the sermons of priests. On Augustine and preaching see Van der Meer, pages 405-467.

CHAPTER   6

Debate with Fortunatus the Manichean

1   In the city of Hippo the Manichean plague had at that time deeply infected many, both citizens and foreigners; they were attracted to it and being led astray by one Fortunatus, a priest of that heresy who was residing there and carrying on his activities.

2   Meanwhile, the Christian citizens and foreigners of Hippo, Catholics and Donatists[1] alike, went to their priest Augustine and asked him to meet the Manichean priest, whom they regarded as a learned man, and to discuss the Law of God[2] with him.   3 Augustine was ready, as the scripture says, to give answer to all who asked the reason for his faith and hope in God (1 Peter 3:15), and quite able to encourage people in sound doctrine and refute its opponents (Titus 1:9). He did not refuse the request, therefore, but asked whether the other was also ready.

4   The petitioners went straight to Fortunatus with the message, and requested and urged and demanded that he also not refuse. But Fortunatus had already known Saint Augustine in Carthage when the latter was still caught in the same error, and he now feared such a meeting.   5 Compelled however by the insistence of his own followers and by shame as well, he promised to meet Augustine in person and engage him in debate.

6   They met therefore at the appointed time and place[3] in the presence of a great many interested people and a throng of the curious. The stenographers opened their notebooks,[4] and the debate began that day and ended on the next.

7   According to the record, the Manichean teacher was unable either to refute the Catholic arguments or to prove that the Manichean sect was based on truth. When his final

answer failed, he went on to say that he would discuss with his superiors the arguments he had not been able to refute; if even they could not give him satisfaction on these points, he would take heed for his own soul. Thus all who had thought of him as a great and learned man could now see that he was utterly unable to make a case for his sect.

8   After being shown up in this way, Fortunatus left Hippo and never returned. Thus, due to our man of God the hearts of all who had been present or who had learned of the event were freed from the Manichean error and were penetrated and conquered by the genuine Catholic faith.

Notes

1.   The Donatists derived their name either from the originator of the schism: Donatus, Bishop of Casae Nigrae, or, more probably, from another Donatus, Bishop of Carthage, who was its most authoritative and energetic leader. Both men were active in Africa in the first half of the fourth century and cut themselves off from the unity of the Church by professing erroneous doctrines on the constitution of the Church and on the sacraments and by causing serious and frequent disturbances. See Willis (in bibliography); Van der Meer, pages 79-117; Frend (in bibliography), especially pages 227-243.

2.   As is clear from chapter 19 of the minutes which Augustine published under the title of *Debate with Fortunatus the Manichean,* the debate focused on the basic tenets of Manicheanism; Augustine summed these up later on as concerned with the problem of the origin of evil (*Revisions* I, 16, 1). The "Law" was discussed at times on the second day (chapters 21-22). But perhaps Possidius is referring here to the broader question of the Old Testament, which was so often the subject of controversy between Manicheans and Catholics.

3.   On 28 and 29 August 392, at the Baths of Sossius; see the beginning of the minutes.

4.   The wax-covered tablets on which the stenographers wrote were held together by cords or rings, like the pages of a book. The use of stenographers (*notarii*) in debates or in important public addresses was widespread, as is clear from other passages in Possidius (14, 6; 16, 1). 7, 3 shows that in addition to official stenographers others might be employed by private individuals.

CHAPTER 7

He Aids the Church by His Speaking and Writing

1 In private and in public, at home and in the church Augustine was preaching and teaching the word of salvation (Acts 13:26) with complete freedom (Acts 4:29) against all the African heretics, especially the Donatists, the Manicheans, and the pagans. He did so in carefully wrought books and in extemporaneous addresses and to the utter admiration and praise of Christians, who did not remain silent about all this but noised it abroad wherever they could.

2 The result was that by the grace of God the Catholic Church of Africa began to lift its head after having long been prostrated, led astray, weighed down and oppressed, while the heretics were growing stronger, especially the Donatists who were rebaptizing the majority of Africans.

3 These books and sermons, which flowed from the marvelous grace of God who inspired him, were filled with abundant arguments and based on the authority of the sacred scriptures. Even the heretics joined the Catholics in listening to him with great enthusiasm, and anyone who wished and had the means could have his words taken down by stenographers.

4 From Hippo this outstanding doctrine and the sweet fragrance of Christ (2 Corinthians 2:15; Ephesians 5:2) were diffused and made known throughout Africa, and the Church overseas rejoiced when it heard of this. For just as all the members suffer when one of them is hurt, so all the members rejoice when one of them is honored (1 Corinthians 12:26).

Ordination of Augustine as bishop by Jaime Huguet (1415-1492), Catalunya Art Museum, Barcelona, Spain.

CHAPTER 8

He Is Unwillingly Ordained
Coadjutor Bishop of Hippo

1   The blessed old man Valerius rejoiced more than anyone at all this and thanked God for the special blessing that had been bestowed on him. Being only human, however, he began to fear that Augustine might be sought out and taken from him to be bishop in another Church that had lost its own. That indeed is precisely what would have happened if Valerius, on discovering such a plan, had not seen to it that Augustine withdrew to a secret location and thus prevented his being found by those who were looking for him.

2   This incident increased the venerable old man's fears. Realizing, moreover, that he himself had been greatly weakened by bad health and age, he secretly wrote to the bishop of Carthage,[1] primate of all Africa, and, alleging his bodily weakness and the burdens of age, asked him that Augustine might be ordained a bishop for the Church of Hippo. What he wanted however was not so much a successor as a fellow bishop here and now. His wish and insistent request elicited a favorable answer.

3   He now asked Megalius, Bishop of Calama[2] and at that time Primate of Numidia, to pay a visit to the Church of Hippo. Bishop Valerius now revealed his unexpected plan to the other bishops who happened to be present,[3] and to all the clergy and people of Hippo. All who heard him expressed their joy and shouted enthusiastically that it should be done, but our priest refused to go against the practice of the Church and accept the episcopate while his own bishop was still living.   4 Appealing to instances in Churches abroad and in Africa, they tried to convince him that this was in fact common practice. He finally yielded to pressure and accepted ordination to the higher rank.[4]

5   Later on, however, Augustine said both orally and in writing[5] that they should not have ordained him a bishop in the lifetime of his own bishop, because it had been forbidden by a general council,[6] although he himself became aware of this only after his ordination. Nor did he want to see done to others what he regretted had been done to him. He therefore worked to have episcopal councils[7] decree that ordaining bishops must make known to priests, whether ordained or to be ordained, all episcopal statutes concerning them.

Notes

1.   Aurelius was Bishop of Carthage from 391 to about 430. Confirmation of elections was usually sought from the primate and was all the more necessary in this case because, as Possidius goes on to remind his readers, the ancient (but often not followed) custom that was reaffirmed in the eighth canon of Nicaea permitted only one bishop in any city. As Augustine wrote a short time later to Paulinus and Terasia (Letter 31, 4), it was precisely the exceptions that induced him (ignorant as he was at the time of the formal conciliar prohibition) to yield to the entreaties of Valerius.

2.   Megalius, Possidius' own predecessor as bishop, died in 397. He was initially opposed to Augustine's ordination as bishop, because (it seems) he believed an accusation of erotic witchcraft which the Donatists falsely brought against Augustine; he quickly changed his mind, however.

3.   They were gathered for a local council.

4.   Opinions vary on the precise date: the beginning of 395; June or July of 395; at the end of 396 (Valerius died in the following year).

5.   In Letter 213, 4, which records the election of Eraclius as coadjutor and successor of Augustine, but with the condition that he not be actually ordained until after Augustine's death.

6.   Council of Nicaea, canon 8. In Hefele and Leclercq, *Histoire des conciles* I, 1, pages 576ff., it is pointed out that in his Letter 213 Augustine reads too much into the canon when he interprets it as forbidding the appointment of coadjutor bishops.

7.   Third Council of Carthage (397), canon 3.

CHAPTER 9

Work for the Conversion of the Donatists

1   As a bishop Augustine preached the word of eternal salvation (Acts 13:26) even more diligently and fervently and with even greater authority than before. And he did so, not in one area only but eagerly and fervently wherever he was asked to go, and the Lord's Church grew and prospered. He was always ready to give seekers an account of his faith and hope in God (see 1 Peter 3:15). The Donatists especially, whether they lived in Hippo or a neighboring town, used to bring his sermons and notes taken at them to their bishops. 2   On hearing of what he had said, these bishops would sometimes issue replies. These, however, were either rejected by their own followers or were reported to the holy Augustine. After studying their answers, he would patiently and gently and, as it is written, with fear and trembling, work for the salvation of all (see Philippians 2:12) by showing that those bishops were not willing or able to refute him and how true and evident on the contrary are the things which the faith of God's Church holds and teaches. All this he did perseveringly day and night.

3   He also wrote letters to eminent bishops of the sect and to lay persons as well, giving his reasons for admonishing and exhorting them either to correct their error or at least to come and debate with him.   4 But these men were not confident of their own cause and were never willing even to answer him; instead they vented their anger and loudly claimed in private and in public that he was a seducer and deceiver of souls. They would say and preach that in defense of the flock he must be killed; having no fear of God or shame before their fellow mortals they even said that God would undoubtedly forgive all the sins of any who could

succeed in doing so. Augustine worked to make everyone aware of their distrust in their own cause, and when they met on public occasions they did not dare to come to grips with him.

CHAPTER 10

Victories and Persecutions

1   In almost all of the Donatist churches there was a novel class of perverse and violent men who professed continence and were known as Circumcellions.[1] There were large throngs of them scattered throughout almost all the districts of Africa.   2 Evil teachers taught them an arrogant boldness and a reckless disregard for law; they spared neither their coreligionists nor outsiders. Against all law and right they interfered in the operation of justice; those who disobeyed them suffered serious losses and injuries, for these men, armed with weapons of all kinds, raged through fields and estates and were not afraid even of shedding blood.   3 Moreover they made war without cause on those who zealously proclaimed the word of God and tried to make peace with these haters of peace (see Psalm 120:7).

4   As truth made headway against their teachings, those who were willing and able broke away from the sect openly or secretly, and gave their allegiance to the peace and unity of the Church, along with any they could bring with them. 5   Seeing their heretical congregations decreasing in numbers, and envious of the growth of the Church, the Circumcellions were inflamed to utter fury and began an intolerable persecution of those loyal to the unity of the Church; by day and night they attacked even the Catholic bishops and ministers and robbed them of all their goods.   6 They beat and crippled many of God's servants; they threw lime mixed with vinegar in the eyes of some and killed others. As a result, these Donatist rebaptizers came to be hated even by their fellows.

Notes

1.   These were bands of fanatical peasants to whom the Catholics gave the name "Circumcellions" because they went about attacking the *cellae* or isolated farmhouses; see Augustine, *Expositions of the Psalms* 132, 3, where they are also called *circelliones* in scorn; this word, derived from *circellus* ("little ring"), may have been the original form. See Willis 11-13 and *passim* (see the Index). In "Circoncellions d'Afrique," *Dictionnaire d'histoire et de geographie ecclesiastique* 12 (1951) 837-839, J. Ferron approvingly cites a new interpretation of the Circumcellion phenomenon: that the rebellion of these peasants was "an episode in the economic decline of Africa and belongs to the economic history of that that province rather than to its religious history." But Frend 173 calls attention to the phrase "who professed continence" and emphasizes the ascetical tendencies of the movement, which he understands as a preparation for martyrdom.

CHAPTER   11

The Monastery of Hippo, a Forge of Apostles
Writings of Augustine

1   While the divine teachings were achieving success, some
of the men who were serving God in the monastery with and
under the direction of holy Augustine began to be ordained
clerics for the Church of Hippo.   2 Thus the truth of the
preaching of the Catholic Church became daily better
known and more evident, and so did the way of life of these
holy servants of God with their continence and austere
poverty. Other Churches therefore began eagerly to ask and
obtain bishops and clerics from the monastery that owed its
origin and growth to this memorable man, with the result
that the Church was established and consolidated in peace
and unity.

3   I myself know of about ten holy and venerable men of
continence and learning, some of them quite outstanding,
whom blessed Augustine gave upon request to the various
churches.[1] These men, inspired by the ideals of that holy
community and being now scattered among the Churches
of the Lord, founded monasteries in their turn; as zeal for the
spread of God's word increased, they prepared brothers for
the priesthood and then advanced them to other Churches.

4   The Church's teaching on saving faith, hope, and love
thus became known through many and among many, not
only in all parts of Africa but also in regions overseas.[2] By
means of published books, which were translated into
Greek,[3] all this teaching was able, with God's help, to make
its way from this one man and through him to many.

5   Consequently, as it is written, sinners saw and were
angered; they gnashed their teeth and wasted away (see
Psalm 112:10). But your servants, as it is said, kept peace

with those who hated peace, and when they spoke they were attacked without cause (Psalm 120:7).

Notes

1.   In addition to Possidius himself and Alypius of Thagaste, who had already been a close friend and follower of Augustine when the latter was professor of rhetoric, we know of Severus of Milevi (Augustine, Letter 31, 9, where he also mentions Peregrinus, a deacon who had come from the monastery of Hippo), Urbanus of Sicca (Letter 149, 34), Evodius of Uzalis, Profuturus of Cirta, Privatus, and Servilius (Letter 33, 2; 158, 9 and 11), Paul of Cataqua (Letter 85, 1), Anthony of Fussala (Letter 209, 3).

2.   This statement is very important, for it shows Augustine to have been restorer of the African Church, and indeed not of the African alone.

3.   This statement too is noteworthy as pointing to a rare phenomenon, since the Greeks usually did not think they had anything to learn from the Latins. We know from other sources that the work *The Acts of Pelagius* was translated into Greek; Possidius probably has this alone in mind even though he uses a rhetorical plural.

CHAPTER 12

Attacks on Augustine and Possidius

1   At times the armed Circumcellions even lay in wait by the roads for the servant of God, Augustine, when he happened to be going by invitation to visit, instruct, and exhort Catholic congregations — something he did quite frequently.   2 On one occasion, though out in full force, they missed their prey, because by the providence of God who used the error of a guide the bishop and his companions reached their destination by a different route; he learned later on that because of this mistake he had escaped the hands of the wicked, and he and all the others gave thanks to God their deliverer. As the public records show, the Circumcellions typically spared neither laity nor clerics.
3   In this context I must not pass over what this man, so illustrious in the Church, undertook and carried through by his diligence and his zeal for God's house[1] against the Donatist rebaptizers.   4 As one of those bishops[2] whom he had sent forth from among the clergy of his monastery was visiting the diocese of Calama that had been entrusted to his care, and for the peace of the Church was preaching what he had learned in opposition to this heresy, it happened that midway on his journey he ran into an ambush set by the Circumcellions. He and his companions escaped, but they were robbed of their animals and baggage, and the bishop himself was seriously injured and wounded.   5 The defender of the Church,[3] who had the law on his side,[4] would not remain silent lest the peace and growth of the Church be further hindered. As a result, Crispinus, the Donatist bishop of Calama and the neighboring region, a well-known, elderly, and learned man, was sentenced to pay a fine in gold as prescribed in the laws of the state against heretics.[5]   6 He

objected, however, appeared before the proconsul, and denied he was a heretic. The defender of the Church withdrew from the case,[6] and it became necessary for the Catholic bishop to represent the opposition and prove that Crispinus really was what he denied being. For if the latter succeeded in hiding his real character, the ignorant might assume from his denial that the Catholic bishop was the real heretic; Augustine's failure to appear would thus have been an occasion of scandal to the weak (see 1 Corinthians 8:9; Romans 14:13).

7 At the insistence, therefore, of Bishop Augustine of esteemed memory, these two bishops of Calama met for debate (this was the third clash between the two on the differences between their communions). A great multitude of Christians in Carthage and throughout Africa waited upon the outcome of the case. In a written judgment of the proconsul Crispinus was declared a heretic. 8 But the Catholic bishop intervened with the judge for him and asked that the fine not be applied; this favor was granted him. The ungrateful Donatist however appealed to the most merciful sovereign, but the required response to the petition brought this answer: it was decreed that the Donatist heretics should not be allowed to exist anywhere and that they were everywhere to be bound by all the laws passed against heretics.[7] The decree also obliged the judge and the court and Crispinus himself each to pay a fine of ten pounds of gold for not having earlier required the fine of Crispinus. But the Catholic bishops, and especially Augustine of sacred memory, promptly took steps to have the ruler pardon all three and withdraw the sentence; this was accomplished with the Lord's help. The Church's growth was greatly advanced by this vigilance and holy zeal.

Notes

1. Psalm 69(68):10; John 2:17. This incident, which Augustine mentions in his *Handbook on Faith, Hope, and Charity* 17, 19, occurred in 404.

2. The bishop in question is Possidius himself, who modestly conceals his name. The same incident is narrated in greater detail by Augustine in

Letter 105, 4, and especially in his *Against Cresconius* 3, 50-52. See Willis 50.

3.   The *defensor* (or *advocatus*) *Ecclesiae* was usually a layman, appointed by the emperor after nomination by the bishop; he represented the Church and churchmen before courts and magistrates.

4.   The reference seems to be specifically to the law promulgated by Theodosius on 15 June 392, which levied a fine of ten pounds of gold against heretics who ordained clerics or accepted clerical office; see the *Theodosian Code* XVI, 5, 21.

5.   Ten pounds of gold, in accordance with the law mentioned in note 4; see Augustine, Letter 105, 4; *Against Cresconius* 3, 51.

6.   As a layman, he had no competence to pronounce in doctrinal matters.

7.   Other incidents besides the one recounted here led the Catholic episcopate to ask the emperor to apply the laws against heretics to the Donatists, who engaged in every kind of violence; this application was made in a series of decrees (*Theodosian Code* XVI, 5, 37-38; 6, 4-5; 11, 2). See Willis 50; Frend, *passim*.

Augustine presides at the conference of bishops in Carthage, North Africa (Bolswert Engravings, 1624).

CHAPTER 13

Growth in Unity and Peace

1   For all that Augustine had done for the peace of the Church
the Lord gave him the palm in this life and stored up a crown
of righteousness for him in heaven (2 Timothy 4:8). Meanwhile, with Christ's help, unity in peace and the brotherhood
of God's Church *grew and multiplied* (see Acts 12:24).

2   This was especially true after the conference at which all the
Catholic bishops met with the Donatist bishops in Carthage[1] at
the command of the most glorious and devout emperor Honorius. The emperor also sent Marcellinus, a secretary at the
court, to be his representative and act as judge in the matter.[2]

3 In this debate the Donatists were utterly refuted by the
Catholics and shown to be in error, and were then sentenced
by the judge; the wicked appealed, but in the answer of the
most benevolent ruler they were condemned as heretics.

4   As a result a greater number than usual of their bishops,
clergy, and people returned to communion and, because
they were now at peace with the Church, had to endure
numerous persecutions from the Donatists, including even
the loss of limb or life. And this entire good work was begun
and carried to completion by that holy man, with the
approval and cooperation of our fellow bishops.[3]

Notes

1.   1-8 June 411. See Willis, 70-76; Frend, 275-289.

2.   Augustine dedicated several of his works to Marcellinus: *The Merits
and Forgiveness of Sins* (411), *The Spirit and the Letter* (probably at the end of
412), and *The City of God* (413).

3.   Possidius may be referring to the seven representatives chosen by the
Catholic bishops; see the Introduction to this translation. According to
Frend, "the unity which Augustine restored [in the struggle with the
Donatists] was deceptive and short-lived" (242).

Frend, "the unity which Augustine restored [in the struggle with the Donatists] was deceptive and short-lived" (242).

Augustine defends the true faith by Jaime Huguet (1415-1492), Catalunya Art Museum, Barcelona, Spain.

CHAPTER 14

Defeat of the Donatist Bishop Emeritus

1 After the conference with the Donatists there were some who claimed that the judge hearing the case had not allowed their bishops to offer a full defense of their cause, because he himself was a Catholic and favored his Church.[1] 2 This, however, was simply an excuse to cover up their complete rout. After all, even before the debate the heretics knew that the judge was a Catholic, and when he sent them a public summons to attend the conference, they promised they would, whereas had they suspected him they could have refused.

3 By a dispensation of almighty God, Augustine of revered memory found himself in Caesarea in Mauretania[2] whither letters from the Apostolic See had ordered him and some of his fellow bishops to go and settle other ecclesiastical problems.[3] 4 On this occasion, as it happened, he met Emeritus, the Donatist bishop of that city and a man whom his followers regarded as the most effective defender of their sect at the conference in Carthage.[4] On this very point Augustine debated with him publicly in church and in the presence of a congregation from both communions; appealing to the official records of the conference, he urged him that if, as his party claimed, he had more to say at the conference but was not allowed to say it, he should not hesitate to say it now when there was no official or other authority present to prevent him; here in his own city and in front of his fellow townsmen let him not refuse freely to defend his own communion. 5 But he was not moved to do so either by this exhortation or by the insistence of his relatives and fellow townsmen, who promised they would return to his communion,[5] though it would mean risking

their property and temporal well-being, if he could refute the Catholic claims.   6 But he was neither willing nor able to say anything more than was in the acts of the conference; he simply kept repeating: "It is already clear from the minutes of the meeting of the bishops in Carthage whether I won or was defeated."[6]

7   On another occasion,[7] the secretary warned him to reply, but he said only "Do as you wish"; his silence made clear to all his lack of confidence in his position, and the Church of God grew and was more firmly established.

8   Those desirous of appreciating more fully the zeal shown by Augustine of blessed memory in laboring for the Church of God may read the minutes of that encounter. They will find there the number and kind of arguments with which Augustine challenged and exhorted that learned, eloquent, and well-known man to say whatever he wished in defense of his party, and they will see how the latter suffered defeat.

Notes

1.   See Augustine, *Proceedings with Emeritus* 2.

2.   The modern Cherchel (or Shershel), on the coast about 100 kilometers (50 miles) west of Algiers; it was the capital of the province of Mauretania Caesariensis.

3.   Augustine speaks of this journey in Letter 190, 1; 193, 1. He undertook it on behalf of Pope Zosimus, but does not say what his business there was. The "fellow bishops," in addition to Deuterius, Metropolitan of Caesarea, and the other bishops of that province, were Alypius of Thagaste, Possidius, Rusticus of Cartenna, Palladius of Tigava, and others who are not named; see *Proceedings with Emeritus* 1.

4.   One of the seven whom the Donatist bishops had chosen to represent them and defend their case; see Augustine, *Revisions* 2, 51.

5.   As Augustine says (*Proceedings with Emeritus* 2), almost all the Donatists of Caesarea had re-entered the Catholic communion.

6.   The reply as given in the minutes of the discussion (*Proceedings with Emeritus* 3) is more complete: "The minutes show whether I have been defeated or have won; and whether I have been defeated by the truth or overwhelmed by force."

7.   If the passage is thus understood, Possidius would seem to be in error. Here is how the facts stand as reported in the document to which he refers the reader in section 8 (below) but which he must not have had

before him as he was writing (as is clear from the way in which he cites Emeritus' reply; see note 6). On 17 September 418, Augustine and Emeritus met in the square, and Emeritus readily entered a church at Augustine's invitation. The latter hoped that Emeritus, like almost all the other Donatists, would be willing to return to the Catholic communion. In fact, however, he elicited from him only a few ambiguous words and became convinced that the man was a stubborn schismatic. Augustine then addressed an exhortation to the people; a further meeting was arranged for Friday, the 19th, in the main basilica. It was at the latter meeting that Emeritus gave the answer which Possidius has just quoted, in a variant form, in section 6; Augustine then asked him: "Why, then, have you come here?"; Emeritus answered: "To reply to your questions"; Augustine insisted and at this point Emeritus said to the secretary: "Just do it" (that is, "write it down"). Augustine says nothing about any admonition by the secretary; Possidius probably inferred the admonition from Emeritus' answer. See Willis, 81f.; Frend, 294-296.

Augustine converts Firmus (Wandereisen Engravings, 1631).

CHAPTER 15

Augustine Digresses and Firmus Sees the Light

1 I recall, as do other brothers and fellow servants who were living with us and that holy man in the Church of Hippo, how on one occasion when we were at table together, he said: 2 "You will have noticed that when I was preaching in the church today I began and ended differently than usual: I did not explain fully the subject I had proposed but left it hanging." 3 We answered: "Yes, we did notice and we remember being surprised." He went on: "I think the reason was that the Lord, in whose hands we and our words are (Wisdom 7:16), intended that some straying member of the congregation should be taught and healed by my distraction and my wandering from the point. 4 It was when I was dealing with certain aspects of my proposed topic that I digressed and veered off into another subject; I did not fully explain and conclude my topic but ended up arguing against the errors of the Manicheans, though I had no intention of saying anything at all about this."

5 A day or two later, if I remember correctly, a businessman named Firmus came and in our presence threw himself on his knees at the feet of holy Augustine, who was sitting in the monastery. The man was weeping as he asked the bishop to join the saints in interceding with the Lord for his, Firmus', sins. He confessed that he had been a Manichean and had lived in that sect for many years and that consequently he had wasted a very great deal of money on the Manicheans and their "Elect," as they are known. But, a few days earlier in the church, he had been converted by God's mercy and Augustine's arguments and had become a Catholic. 6 Venerable Augustine and the rest of us who were present

71

carefully inquired what it was specifically in the sermon that had satisfied him. When he told us, and we recalled the sequence of thoughts in that discourse, we were filled with wonder and dumbfounded at God's profound plan for human salvation. We praised and blessed his holy name (Psalm 102:1), because he brings about the salvation of souls when and as he wills and by whatever instruments he wills, whether or not these realize what they are doing.[1]

7   From that time forward Firmus abandoned his business and made his own the way of life of the servants of God. He made progress as a member of the Church and in another country was asked and indeed compelled to became a priest by God's will. He kept meanwhile to his holy way of life and is perhaps still living in this world overseas.

Notes

1.   Possidius may have had in mind here the passage in *Confessions* 6, 7, 12, in which Augustine tells how a comparison he himself had happened to make in the course of a lecture delivered Alypius from his passions for the spectacles in the arena.

CHAPTER 16

He Unmasks and Converts Manicheans

1   It happened in Carthage that a man named Ursus, a Catholic and an administrator in the royal palace, came upon some of the male and female Manicheans known as the "Elect"; he took them to the church, where they were questioned by the bishops in the presence of stenographers.[1] 2   Among the bishops was Augustine of holy memory, a man who had a better knowledge than anyone else of that accursed sect. Citing passages from books which the Manicheans themselves accepted, he laid bare their horrible blasphemies and persuaded them to confess them. The ecclesiastical records also make clear, from the confession of these "elect" women, the base and shameful things they are accustomed to doing among themselves.   3   The vigilance of pastors thus helped the Lord's flock to grow and provided an appropriate defense against thieves and robbers.

4   Augustine also debated publicly in the Church of Hippo with a certain Felix, who was likewise one of the Manichean "Elect"; the people were present and stenographers took down what was said. After the second or third session the Manichean, seeing the emptiness and error of his sect unmasked, converted to our faith and Church, as can be seen by consulting the record.[2]

Notes

1.   This examination, which Augustine reports in greater detail in his *Heresies*, 46, took place in 421.

2.   *The Debate with Felix the Manichean*, in two books, is published among the works of Augustine. The date of the meeting is indicated at the beginning of the record: 7 December 404. After the first debate, the continuation was put off until 12 December.

Augustine the teacher by Jaime Huguet (1415-1492), Catalunya Art Museum, Barcelona, Spain.

CHAPTER 17

Debates with Two Arians, Pascentius and Maximinus

1 There was also a certain Pascentius, a count in the royal palace[1] and an Arian. As an extremely energetic collector of imperial taxes he used his authority for a cruel and unrelenting attack on the Catholic faith. He employed biting wit and his official powers to harass and disturb many priests of God who were living lives of simple faith. Through the mediation of some honored[2] men of noble rank he challenged Augustine to a public meeting in Carthage. 2 The heretic adamantly refused, however, to allow notebook and pen to be present before and during the meeting, as our teacher urgently wished. He feared the laws of the state, he said, and did not want to endanger himself by having anything in writing.[3] When Augustine saw that his episcopal colleagues present wanted a private and unrecorded debate to be held, he agreed, but he predicted what in fact did happen: that since there would be no record, everyone would be free after the meeting to claim that he had said what he had not and that he had not said what he had.
3 Augustine joined in the debate; he stated what he believed, and listened to the other's tenets. Using solid arguments and the authority of scripture he explained and demonstrated the foundations of our faith; he also explained and refuted the claims of Pascentius as having no basis in truth or in the authority of the sacred scriptures.
4 When the two parties to the debate had gone their ways, Pascentius grew increasingly enraged. He threw out many lies in defense of his erroneous faith and proclaimed that he had defeated the widely acclaimed Augustine. 5 All this could not be kept quiet, and Augustine was forced to write to

Pascentius,[4] although he omitted the names of the disputants out of respect for Pascentius' fears.[5] In these letters he gave a faithful account of what the two sides had said and done; he was ready to prove the accuracy of his account, if it were denied, by numerous witnesses, namely, the honored men of rank who were present at the meeting.   6 To these two letters Pascentius for his part sent an answer that hardly deserved the name. In it he was able only to offer insults rather than a defense of his sect. This is attested by those willing and able to read.[6]

7   At the desire and request of many, and in the presence of eminent persons, Augustine also debated at Hippo[7] with one Maximinus, an Arian bishop who had come to Africa with the Goths;[8] the statements of both sides were taken down in writing.[9]   8 If those interested will read the record carefully, they will surely discover the claims which this clever but irrational heresy uses to attract and deceive, as well as what the Catholic Church holds and preaches about the divine Trinity.   9 After returning from Hippo to Carthage, however, the heretic lied and boasted that because of his vast outpouring of words in the debate he had come away victorious. Those ignorant of the divine law could not easily examine these matters and pass judgment. Later on, therefore, venerable Augustine summed up in writing[10] the individual objections raised and answers given in the course of the entire debate; he showed that Maximinus had been unable to answer the objections raised against him, and added some points which could not be introduced and written down in the limited time available at the conference. As a matter of fact, that malicious fellow had managed to extend his final and by far his lengthiest speech throughout the remaining hours of the day.

Notes

1.   "Count" (*comes*) was a title given to many imperial officials, whose functions were indicated by a further description: "Count in charge of . . ." It could also be a purely honorary title.

2.   In the Late Empire the official title of *Honoratus* was given to citizens who had filled important civil or military offices.

3.   In point of fact, during the morning debate Pascentius had accepted Augustine's invitation to continue the meeting in the afternoon and in the presence of stenographers who would take the minutes; when the time came, however, Pascentius withdrew his assent (Augustine, Letter 238, 1-2.6-7, and 9; Letter 239, which Possidius must have had before him). The date of the meeting, like that of the letters, is uncertain: perhaps about 406.

4.   The two letters mentioned in note 3.

5.   More accurately, he omitted only Pascentius' name, but gave his own name and that of Alypius; see Letter 238, 4, 26, 27, and 28.

6.   Pascentius' letter, which has come down to us among the letters of Augustine (Letter 240), is indeed insulting in its tone; Augustine sent a calm and objective reply (Letter 241).

7.   According to Tillemont, the most probable date for the conference is 428; but Zarb correctly notes that the chronological indication given by Prosper in his *Chronicle* for 427 obliges us to say that it took place in that year.

8.   This is probably the Maximinus who composed a *Dissertation against Ambrose* (383) and various other writings (about 40 sermons and three pieces of polemics), which have come down to us under other names and especially as the work of Saint Maximus of Turin. See E. Dekkers, *Clavis Patrum Latinorum* (Third edition; Steenbrugge: Abbatia Sancti Petri), nos. 692ff.

9.   In the *Debate with Maximinus, an Arian Bishop* (PL 42:709-742).

10.   In his *Two Books against Maximinus, a Heretic and Arian Bishop* (PL 42:743-814). As Possidius says below, at the end of the debate Maximinus deliberately dragged out his final speech in order that Augustine might have no time to answer; the latter therefore proposed that the meeting continue the next day; Maximinus refused, claiming his return to Carthage was urgently needed. Augustine then pledged himself to put in writing the answer he had not had time to give orally, and Maximinus promised to reply to each point. Augustine kept his promise, but his adversary did not.

Augustine with the Emperor Honorius (Bolswert Engravings, 1624).

CHAPTER 18

Opposition to the Pelagians

Fruits of His Labors

Writings

1   Against the Pelagians too, those new heretics of our time,[1] Augustine labored for almost ten years.[2] They were skillful debaters and still more subtle and destructive in their writings and in the talking they did everywhere, in public and in people's homes. Augustine composed and published numerous books against them and preached very frequently to the people in church regarding that error.   2 And because these perverse men were attempting by flattery to have their heresy accepted by the Apostolic See, African councils of holy bishops[3] urgently tried to convince the holy pope of the City, first the venerable Innocent and then his successor, the holy Zosimus, that this sect deserved to be abhorred and condemned by believing Catholics.   3 The bishops of that great see did in fact at various times brand these men as heretics and cut them off from the members of the Church. They sent letters to the African Churches of both West and East, decreeing that they were to be anathematized and shunned by all Catholics.[4]

4   Furthermore, the devout Emperor Honorius, after hearing of the judgment pronounced on these men by the Catholic Church, likewise condemned them in his laws and decreed that they were to be regarded as heretics.[5]   5 Some of them therefore returned to the bosom of holy Mother Church, from which they had withdrawn; others are still returning, as the truth of the orthodox faith becomes better known and prevails over that detestable error.

6   That memorable man, Augustine, a leading member of the Lord's body,[6] was always solicitous and most vigilant for the good of the universal Church.   7   And God granted him the enjoyment, even in this life, of the fruits of his labors, first in the diocese of Hippo, which had been especially entrusted to him and in which he established unity and peace, and then also in other parts of Africa. There he saw the Church put forth buds and increase, whether through his personal efforts or through those of others, including men whom he had sent to those Churches as their bishops. He also had the joy of seeing the Manicheans, Donatists, Pelagians, and pagans largely disappear and become members of God's Church.   8   He also fostered the undertakings and zeal of all and took delight in everything good. He showed a kind and holy toleration of less disciplined brethren and lamented the wickedness of evil men, whether within the Church or outside of it. For, as I said, the gains made by the Lord always gave him joy, while the losses saddened him.

9   So many are the works he dictated and published, so many the sermons he preached in church and then wrote down and revised — whether directed against heretics or devoted to interpreting the canonical books for the building up of the Church's holy children — that even a student would hardly have the energy to read and become acquainted with all of them.   10   Nevertheless, in order not to cheat in any way those who are eager for the word of truth, I have decided to append to the present little work a short list of those books, sermons, and letters. In this way, those who love God's truth more than temporal riches will be able to choose the ones they wish to read and become acquainted with; then they may apply to the Church of Hippo to make a copy, or they may visit the library in Hippo, where they may find more correct copies, or may make inquiry wherever they can, and, having found what they want, may make a copy and keep it, and generously allow others to copy it in turn.[7]

Notes

1.   Pelagius, a Breton monk, denied the necessity of God's grace and replaced revealed Christianity with a system of rationalistic naturalism.

2.   Augustine was engaged in the struggle with Pelagianism from 411, when he published his three books on *The Merits and Forgiveness of Sins*, to the close of his life. Some scholars think that when Possidius speaks of "ten years" he is looking upon the battle as won when Pope Zosimus issued the first condemnation of Pelagianism in his *Epistola tractoria* of 418. This explanation seems unacceptable for two reasons: first, the biographer could not have overlooked the many antipelagian writings of the period after 418; second, since 411, when Pelagius landed in Africa, must be the starting point, Possidius' "almost ten years" is hardly still applicable. Another forced explanation is that Possidius is here thinking only of the major antipelagian works, which appeared in rapid succession from 412 to 421, and not of those published, after an interval, between 426 and 429. The only explanation left is that the text has been altered by the dropping of an "X" and that it should read "XX" (twenty) and not "X" (ten). If Possidius actually wrote "XX" he would be in substantial agreement with Prosper who, writing between 432 and 434, says that the Catholic army had been fighting for twenty or more years, under Augustine's leadership, against the enemies of God's grace.

3.   In 411 or 412 a Council of Carthage had already condemned Caelestius; in 416 Caelestius and Pelagius were condemned at the Council of Carthage and then at the Council of Milevi. Another assembly seems to have met in Carthage in the autumn of 417 to study the letter in which Pope Zosimus favored Pelagius (see note 4). Still another council was held on 1 May 418, at which the bishops took formal note of the same pope's subsequent condemnation of the heretics and formulated Catholic teaching on original sin and grace.

4.   Pope Innocent did so in a letter of 27 January 417 (Letter 182 among the letters of Augustine). Pope Zosimus, who succeeded Innocent on 17 March of that same year, initially showed himself vexed by the conduct of the African bishops and undertook to protect Caelestius and Pelagius; but by the spring of 418 he was writing to these same bishops to excommunicate the heresiarchs, and in his *Epistula tractoria*, an encyclical letter to all the Churches, he solemnly condemned the Pelagian heresy.

5.   Edict of 9 June 419, which is Letter 201 among the letters of Augustine.

6.   A Pauline image, very familiar to Augustine, as is the whole Pauline doctrine of the mystical body.

7.   This catalogue, which Possidius himself says in his conclusion is anything but complete, has come down to us.

Part II

Augustine's Everyday Life

(Chapters 19 — 27, 5)

Saint Augustine by Michael Pacher, Alte Pinakothek, Munich, West
Germany.

CHAPTER 19

Augustine as Judge

1   Augustine also obeyed the instruction of the Apostle, who says: *When one of you has a grievance against another, does he dare seek judgment from the wicked and not from the saints? Are you not aware that the saints will judge the world? And if you shall judge the world, are you unworthy to pass judgment in trifling matters? Are you not aware that we shall judge angels? How much more, then, the things of the world! If you have disputes about worldly things among you, appoint as your judges those who count least in the Church! I say this to shame you. Is there no wise person among you who can judge between brother and brother? Must a brother go to court against a brother, and this before unbelievers?* (1 Corinthians 6:1-6).[1]

2   Consequently, whenever Christians or even persons from one or other sect appealed to him,[2] he listened to the case with diligent care, having always in mind the words of the man who said he preferred to judge between people unknown to him rather than between his friends because if he judged equitably between people unknown to him he had a chance of acquiring a friend, whereas in judging between his friends he was sure to lose whichever one he declared to be in the wrong.   3 Sometimes he heard cases right up to the dinner hour, sometimes he fasted the entire day, but he always examined the facts and passed judgment with an eye on the movements of Christian souls, that is, considering how each party was advancing or falling off in faith and morals.   4 He took the opportunity of teaching both parties the truth of God's law and bringing it home to them and of reminding them of the means of obtaining eternal life. The only return he sought for the sacrifice of his time was the Christian obedience and devotion that is owed

to God and one's fellow human beings. Sinners he rebuked in the presence of all, so that the rest might learn to fear (see 1 Timothy 5:20).   5 In all this he thought of himself as a watchman set by the Lord over the house of Israel (Ezekiel 3:17; 33:7); he preached the word in season and out of season, convincing, exhorting, rebuking, and teaching with unfailing patience (2 Timothy 4:2), and taking special care to teach in turn those fitted for teaching others (2 Timothy 2:2). 6   When asked by some to take a hand in their temporal concerns, he wrote letters to various persons for them,[3] but he regarded this occupation as a kind of forced labor that took him away from more important things. His real delight was to speak of the things of God, whether in public addresses or at home in familiar converse with his brothers.

Notes

1.   Augustine cites this passage in rebuking the faithful in *Expositions of the Psalms* 80, 21 and *Handbook on Faith, Hope, and Charity* 78.

2.   According to G. Bardy, *Saint Augustin. L'homme et l'oeuvre* (Paris: Bibliotheque Augustinienne, 1940[3]), 179, "it was natural that the bishops should at all times serve as judge for the faithful, and Emperor Constantine had officiously acknowledged their jurisdiction over the members of their dioceses. He had gone even further and authorized all litigants, Christian or non-Christian, to have recourse to the episcopal court if they thought this appropriate. Later laws had further defined the competence of these courts, limiting it somewhat in the process. Despite this, the episcopal courts were not any the less frequented at the end of the fourth and beginning of the fifth century by a throng of people who preferred its speedy and simplified procedures to the often prolonged and expensive formalities of the civil courts." Augustine often laments the burden of this office, or at least alludes to it; see, for example, *The Work of Monks* 37 (published in about 400), where he again cites, in part, 1 Corinthians 6:1-6; the sermon referred to in Letter 213 (from the year 426); *Expositions of the Psalms* 25, 13; 118, 24, 3; Letter 33, 5; 48, 1; Sermon 355, 3; and see Van der Meer 258-261.

3.   This was the purpose of Letters 113-116. To see what this work of charity cost the bishop and the spirit in which he did it see Sermon 302, 17. In any case, bishops regarded this kind of "intercession" as a pastoral duty; see Ennodius, *Life of Saint Epiphanius* 50.

CHAPTER 20

Dealings with the Authorities

1   We know, too, that when persons very dear to him asked him for letters of petition to the civil authorities he refused. He chose, he said, to follow the principle of a wise man of whom it was reported that regard for his own reputation kept him from doing many favors for friends. Augustine added that authorities who grant favors usually become importunate.

2   When he did decide that he ought to mediate, he did it in such an honorable and restrained way that, far from seeming a burden and annoyance to the authorities, he even roused their admiration. On one occasion, for example, in a case of necessity he intervened in writing for people who were petitioning a vicar for Africa named Macedonius.[1] The latter granted the favor and sent this answer:

3   "I greatly admire your wisdom as shown both in the works you have published and in this letter of recommendation which you have not felt it too much trouble to send for someone in distress.   4 The published works display an unsurpassable insight, knowledge, and holiness, and this letter such modesty that if, deservedly venerated Lord and esteemed Father, I did not grant your request, I would feel the fault lay in myself and not in the favor asked.   5 For you do not insist, as most men in your position do, on extorting from me whatever the distressed parties want. Rather, you suggest what you think may be asked from a judge beset by so many cares, and you do it with that accommodating modesty that is so effective in settling difficulties among good people. Therefore I immediately granted the desire of those you recommended; for I had given you reason to expect that I would."

Notes

1.   Macedonius was head of the Roman "diocese" of Africa. As is clear from the exchange of letters (Letters 152 and 154 among the letters of Augustine were written by Macedonius; Letters 153 and 155 by Augustine), the bishop had intervened, probably in 414, in favor of some persons who were under indictment, and Macedonius had immediately granted his wish. Macedonius then asked Augustine for help in resolving a doubt about how the guilty were to be treated; Augustine sent a lengthy answer and received in reply a letter of which Possidius cites approximately the first third here. Along with his letter Augustine had sent Macedonius the first three books of his *The City of God*, which he had written during the previous year. These were the "works" to which Macedonius is referring in the passage cited by Possidius. Macedonius' letter of admiration for the bishop elicited a reply in which the latter rejected the encomium and explained at length in what true wisdom and virtue consist and how they are God's gifts.

CHAPTER   21

Councils and Ordinations

1   He took part whenever he could in the councils which the holy bishops held in various provinces. He looked out not for his own interests but for the interests of Jesus Christ.[1]   2   I mean by this that he labored, for example, to preserve unstained the faith of the holy Catholic Church and to see to it that various priests and clerics who had been rightly or wrongly excommunicated should be either absolved or cast out.   3   When it came to ordaining priests and clerics he believed it his duty to respect the consensus of the majority of Christians[2] and the custom of the Church.

Notes

1.   See 2:21.
2.   This was in accordance with the practice of the Church, a practice confirmed by canon 6 of the Council of Nicaea.

QVISQVIS AMAT DICTIS ABSENTVM RODERE VITAM,
HANC MENSAM VETITAM NOVERIT ESSE SIBI.

Augustine teaches charity: "Let those who like to slander the lives of the absent know that their own are not worthy of this table" (Wandereisen Engravings, 1631).

CHAPTER 22

Simplicity of Life and Freedom of Spirit
Charity Above All

1   His clothing and shoes, and even his bedding, were simple and appropriate, being neither overly fastidious nor slovenly. It is in these externals that people usually go in either for arrogant display or for self-abasement; in either case they seek not the interests of Jesus Christ but their own (see Philippians 2:21). Augustine, however, as I just indicated, followed the middle way and did not deviate to right or left (see Numbers 20:17).[1]

2   His meals were frugal and economical; at times, however, in addition to herbs and vegetables they included meat for the sake of guests[2] or sick brethren. Moreover, they always included wine, for he knew and taught, with the Apostle, that *everything created by God is good, and nothing is to be rejected if it is received with thanksgiving; for then it is consecrated by the word of God and prayer* (1 Timothy 4:4-5).   3   Holy Augustine expressed the same thought in his *Confessions*[3] when he said: "It is the uncleanness of gluttony that I fear, not unclean meat. For I know that Noe was allowed to eat all kinds of meat that were suitable as food (Genesis 9:24); that Elias was fed on meat (1 Kings 17:16); and that John the Baptist, remarkable ascetic though he was, was not polluted by the flesh of living creatures, the locusts which were granted him as food (Matthew 3:4). On the other hand, I know that Esau was defrauded by his greed for a dish of lentils (Genesis 25:29-34); that David reproached himself for longing for a drink of water (2 Samuel 23:15-17); and that Christ our King was tempted not by meat but by bread (Matthew 4:3). And the people in the desert deserved rebuke, not because they wanted meat, but because in their greed for food they sulked

and grumbled against the Lord (Numbers 11:1ff)."   4 As regards the drinking of wine, the Apostle says in his letter to Timothy: *No longer drink only water, but use a little wine for the sake of your stomach and your frequent ailments* (1 Timothy 5:23).[4]

5   Only the spoons were of silver; the vessels in which the food was brought to the table were of earthenware, wood, or marble, and this not by unavoidable poverty but by deliberate policy (Philemon 14).[5]

6   He practiced hospitality at all times. Even at table he found more delight in reading[6] and conversation than in eating and drinking.

To prevent one plague that afflicts social intercourse he had these words inscribed on the table: "Let those who like to slander the lives of the absent know that their own are not worthy of this table."[7] In this way he reminded all his guests that they ought to abstain from unnecessary and harmful gossip.

7   On one occasion, when some fellow bishops, close friends of his, had forgotten the inscription and disobeyed its warning, he rebuked them sternly, being so upset as to say that either the verses must be erased from the table or he would get up from table in the middle of the meal and retire to his room. I and others at that meal witnessed this.

Notes

1.   In Harnack's interpretation, Possidius is here defending Augustine against the charge that his community did not practice the rigorous asceticism customary in monasteries. It is to be noted, however, that the standards of moderation set down here were well known in ascetical teaching (see, for example, Cassian, *Institutes* I, 2) and that with regard to meat and wine in particular Augustine was reacting against the Manichees who forbade their use on the grounds that they had their origin in the evil principle (see, for example, *The Manichean Way of Life* II, 35). A witness to the lively reaction which this teaching aroused even in ascetical circles can be found in the Prologue to *The Lausiac History* of Palladius. The First and Second Councils of Braga (561 and 572) prescribed that clerics who did not eat meat should at least eat vegetables that were cooked together with meat, lest they become suspect of Priscillianism. On life in Augustine's household see Van der Meer, pages 235-241.

2.   Augustine considered it the duty of a bishop to show hospitality to visitors or people passing through; he even gives this as the reason for establishing his monastery right in the episcopal palace, namely, in order that the life of the monastery in the stricter sense of this term might not be disturbed by visitors (see Sermon 355, 2).

3.   *Confessions* 10, 31, 46.

4.   Saint Epiphanius of Pavia likewise justified the moderate use of wine with an appeal to this passage (see Ennodius, *Life of Saint Epiphanius* 48).

5.   Dishes made of silver were fairly common in the imperial age. Of Saint Caesarius of Arles we are likewise told that among his table utensils only the spoons were of silver (*Life of Caesarius of Arles* I, 27).

6.   Cassian, a contemporary of Saint Augustine, attributes the introduction of reading at table to the Cappadocian monks (that is, to Saint Basil, who wrote their Rule) (see Cassian, *Institutes* IV, 17). While at Saint Augustine's table reading alternated with conversation, Saint Caesarius of Arles prescribed uninterrupted reading at dinner and supper; when the reading was finished, some one had to report on what had been read.

7.   Possidius does not say who wrote these two lines of verse, which are also to be found in the *Latin Anthology*, no. 487a. According to some scholars, Augustine tells us that he himself wrote them, but the claim is based on a spurious sermon (To the Brethren in the Desert 26); it is, of course, possible that he did indeed write them.

Augustine gives to the poor by Mathieu de Wayere, from the choir stalls of the Church of Saint Gertrude, Louvain, Belgium — the sculptures date from 1538-1543.

CHAPTER 23

Disinterested Charity

1   He was always mindful of his fellow poor and distributed
to them from the same source on which he and those living
with him depended: the income from the Church's property
and the offerings of the faithful.   2   And if, as often happens,
this property stirred envy of the clergy,[1] he would tell the
people[2] that he would prefer to live on the offerings of God's
people rather than be bothered with the care and administration of the property and that he was ready to renounce
it, so that all the servants and ministers of God might live as
we read in Old Testament, where those who served the altar
shared in the sacrificial offerings (see Deuteronomy 18:1-8;
1 Corinthians 9:13). But the laity were never willing to
follow this course.

Notes

1.   Some have interpreted the passage as referring to envy among the
clergy themselves, who supposedly rebuked the bishop for giving too
much to the poor and too little to them. But the interpretation given here
is the only one that fits the context.
2.   For example, in Sermons 355 and 356.

CHAPTER 24

Administration of the Church's Property

1   The administration of the house attached to the church[1] and of all its possessions he used to delegate to the more capable among the clergy,[2] letting each of them have the task in turn. He never kept the key or wore the ring.[3] Instead, those in charge of the house kept a record of all income and expenditures and gave an account of it to him at the end of the year, so that he might know how much had been received and how much spent, and how much remained to be spent. In many matters he simply took the word of the person in charge and did not require detailed and documented accounts.

2   He refused ever to buy a house or field or villa, but if someone made a spontaneous gift of such to the Church or left it as a legacy, he did not refuse it but ordered its acceptance.   3 We know indeed that he did at times refuse inheritances; the reason, however, was not that they would be useless to the poor but that he thought it only right and just for the children or parents or relatives of the dead to have them, even though the dead had been unwilling to leave them in that way.[4]

4   One of the honored citizens of Hippo, who was then residing in Carthage, wished to give some property to the Church of Hippo; he drew up the deed, in which he reserved only the income for himself, and of his own accord sent it to Augustine of holy memory. The latter gladly accepted the offering and congratulated the man on his concern for his eternal salvation.   5 A few years later, however, when I happened to be living in close association with Augustine, the donor sent his son with a letter asking that the deed be returned to the son and directing that

instead a hundred gold pieces be given to the poor.   6 When the holy man learned of this he was grieved that the donor had either only pretended to make the gift or had repented of his good work. In pain of spirit at this perverse action, he rebuked and chided the man in whatever words God suggested to his heart.   7 He immediately returned the deed, which the man had sent of his own accord without anyone desiring or demanding it, and he spurned the money as well. He also felt bound to rebuke and correct the man in writing, warning him to do humble penance before God for his pretense or wickedness, lest he depart from this world with such a serious sin on his conscience.

8   Augustine often observed that the Church can much more securely and safely accept legacies left by the deceased than inheritances, which are likely to bring anxiety and loss; and that even legacies are to be offered rather than requested.   9   Nor would he himself ever accept property to be held in trust, but he did not forbid clerics willing to do so.

10   He did not allow his heart to become attached to or entangled in the possessions of the Church. But while his attention and concern were focused rather on the more important things of the spirit, he did at times turn his thoughts from eternal things and bring them down to temporal affairs.   11 Once these had been arranged in orderly fashion, he would withdraw from them as from stings and annoyances and return to the interior, higher things of the mind, either studying the things of God or dictating something of what he had discovered or correcting what had been written at his dictation. This he did in laborious days and nights filled with toil.   12 In this he resembled that most devout woman, Mary, who is a type of the heavenly Church and of whom we read that she sat at the Lord's feet and listened intently to his words. And when her sister complained that though she had so much serving to do Mary did not help her, she was told: *Martha, Martha, Mary has chosen the better part, and it shall not be taken from her* (Luke 10:39).[5]

13 Augustine never had any desire for new buildings; he thus avoided any preoccupation with them, for he wanted to keep his soul free of all temporal anxieties. He did not, however, forbid others to build them, provided they were not extravagant.

14 When from time to time the Church was without money, he would tell the Christian people that he had nothing to give to the poor.   15 For the sake of prisoners and a large number of needy people he even ordered the sacred vessels to be broken and melted down.   16 I would not mention this if I did not know that it offends the carnal judgment of some people. But that very course of action is the one that Ambrose of revered memory said and wrote should undoubtedly be followed in such cases of need.[6]
17 At times, too, when speaking to the faithful in church he would admonish them for neglecting the poor box and the collection for the sacristy,[7] which supplied the needs of the altar; on one occasion he told us that in his presence blessed Ambrose had dealt with the same subject in church.

Notes

1.   The reference is to the monastery in which the bishop resided with the clergy who shared common life with him; in Sermon 355, 2, it is called *domus episcopi* or "bishop's house" (according to Lambot's reading; others read *episcopii*).

2.   Canon IV (20) of the Statutes of the Early Church (from Gaul, late fifth century) prescribed that "the bishop is not to take on any of the cares of the house but is to devote himself solely to the word of God and prayer." From what Possidius goes on to say here, it appears that there was a single administrator or steward at a time, who held his office for a year, as in the plan drawn up while Augustine was still in Milan (*Confessions* 4, 14, 24).

3.   A signet ring was used to mark things as one's own or to authenticate signatures on administrative documents.

4.   An instance is cited in Sermon 355, 5. Saint Ambrose taught the same in his *Commentary on Luke* 8, 77, where he based his view on the gospel (Matthew 15:3-6).

5.   See Augustine, Sermon 179, 3.

6.   Ambrose, *The Duties of Ministers* 2, 136ff. The needy to whom reference is made here must have been chiefly Italians forced to flee overseas by the invasions of the Goths. Saint Exuperius, Bishop of

Toulouse, did the same as Augustine when his city was besieged by the Vandals in 408 (Jerome, Letter 125, 20), as did Deogratias, Bishop of Carthage, in order to ransom prisoners of the Vandals and the Moors (Victor of Vita, *History of the Persecution of the Province of Africa* 1, 25). Two bishops of Arles, Saints Hilary (Honoratus?) (*Life of Hilary* 11) and Caesarius (*Life* 1, 32), likewise acted in the same way (though in this matter their biographers adopt a defensive and polemical tone); as, at an earlier date, did Saint Cyril of Jerusalem, who was rebuked for it by an adversary, Acacius of Caesarea (Sozomen, *History of the Church* 4, 25); similar accusations were leveled against Saint John Chrysostom at the Synod of Quercia in 403. On Saint Augustine's concern for the poor see Van der Meer, pages 137-140.

7.   "Poor box" and "sacristy" seem to be the meanings of the two words *gazophylacium* and *secretarium*. See Augustine, *Expositions of the Psalms* 63, 11.

CHAPTER 25

Paternal Authority

The Law of Forgiveness

1 Augustine's clerics, like himself, were fed and clothed from the common funds; together they shared at all times a single house and a single table.[1]

2 Lest any take oaths too readily and perjure themselves,[2] he urged the people in his sermons in church[3] and also taught his followers not to swear, even at table. If anyone slipped and took an oath, he lost one of his allowed drinks[4] (the companions of Augustine's house and table were granted a set number of drinks).[5]

3 Actions contrary to discipline and departures from the rule of uprightness and honorableness Augustine rebuked or let pass as seemed appropriate or necessary. His primary emphasis in these matters was that no one should descend to lies in seeking to excuse his sins.[6]

4 In addition, anyone who, while offering his gift at the altar, remembered that a brother had something against him was to leave his gift at the altar, go to be reconciled with his brother, and then return to offer his gift at the altar (see Matthew 5:23-24). 5 If on the other hand he himself had something against his brother, he was to admonish him in private; if the other listened, he would have gained his brother; if the other refused to listen, he should take one or two others with him; if the other scorned even them, he should have recourse to the Church; and if the other refused to obey even the Church, then they should treat him as a pagan and a tax collector (Matthew 18:15-17). 6 Augustine added that if a brother sinned and asked forgiveness, his failure should be forgiven not seven times but seventy times

seven times (Matthew 18:21-22), just as each one daily asks the Lord for forgiveness (Matthew 6:12).

Notes

1. Augustine goes into greater detail in Sermon 355, 2.

2. See Matthew 5:34ff.; James 5:12. The same reason is given for this prohibition by Saint Augustine (Letter 157, 40) and Saint Ambrose: "Those who make a habit of swearing will inevitably perjure themselves on some occasion" (*Exhortation to Virgins* 74).

3. See an index to Augustine's works under the words *iuratio* and *iurare*. Augustine himself admits that he had had a struggle to rid himself of this habit (Sermons 180, 10; 307, 5), which we know from other sources was widespread at that time; see, for example, Palladius, *Lausiac History* 9; Salvian, *Divine Governance* 3, 31; 4, 68-77; *Statutes of the Early Church*, canon LXXV (61), where the reference is to clerics. One of the first admonitions in the *Rule for Virgins* of Saint Caesarius of Arles is that they are to avoid oaths "and curses as if these were the devil's poison."

4. The historian Harnack thought that this punishment was suggested by the statutes of some secular guild.

5. The same regulation is found in Saint Benedict, *Rule* 40.

6. See Psalm 140(141):4, which Augustine (and therefore Possidius) understood according to the Vulgate (the Hebrew text reads somewhat differently).

CHAPTER 26

Safeguards of Chastity

1   No woman ever frequented his house; no woman ever stayed there, not even his own sister, a widow consecrated to God who ruled the maidservants of the Lord until her death,[1] or his brother's daughters,[2] who were likewise consecrated to the service of God. This despite the fact that the councils of holy bishops had made exceptions for such persons as these.   2 It is true (he used to say) that no suspicion of evil can arise from having a sister or nieces staying in the house. On the other hand, these women must inevitably bring female friends to stay them, and still others would come from outside to visit them, and all this could be a stumbling block and a source of scandal for the weak (see 1 Corinthians 8:9; Romans 14:13). What is more, men who might be staying with the bishop or cleric in question might succumb to very human temptations due to the women living there or visiting (see 1 Corinthians 10:13), or might at least suffer harm to their reputations due to evil suspicions. 3 He therefore said that women should never be allowed to stay in the same house with the servants of God, however chaste the latter might be, lest, as I said, the example given be a source of scandal or a stumbling block to the weak. And if women asked to visit him or even simply to pay their respects, he never received them except in the presence of other clerics, nor did he ever speak with them alone, even if the matter required secrecy.[3]

Notes

1.   We do not know the sister's name. Augustine mentions her in 423, after her death, when writing to some monks to rebuke them for their dissensions and to offer them a rule of life (Letter 211, 4).

2.   The brother's name was Navigius (see above, Chapter 2, note 5).

3.   Saint Jerome prescribed the same safeguards to Nepotian, a cleric (Letter 52, 5), as did Saint Ambrose to all ecclesiastics (*The Duties of Ministers* 1, 87). The Council of Hippo (393), canon 16, and the Third Council of Carthage (397) allowed clerics to have mother, sisters, aunts, nieces, and relatives in general living with them.

Charity and Prudence

Humble and Serene Trust

1   In his own visits he followed the rule of the Apostle, namely, to visit only orphans and widows in need (James 1:27).   2   Or if the sick asked him to visit them, pray to the Lord for them, and lay his hand on them, he would go without delay.   3   He did not visit monasteries of women except in real need.
4   He asserted that in their lives and habits men of God should follow the rules which he himself had learned from the teaching of Ambrose of holy memory: never to seek a wife for someone or to write a recommendation for a man entering upon a military career[1] or to accept invitations to dinner in the locality.[2]   5   The reasons he gave for these rules were as follows: lest spouses quarrel and curse the one who had brought them together (but he also said that when spouses were in agreement, a priest should, if asked, intervene to ratify and bless covenants and consents already made[3]); and lest the man recommended for the military turn out badly and blame his backer; and lest the habit of temperance be lost through frequent attendance at banquets with fellow townsmen.

Notes

1.   Perhaps it would be preferable to take this as a reference to public office generally rather than to the military in particular, in keeping with a use of *militare* and *militia* that was common at this period. See, for example, Augustine, *Confessions* 6, 14f., where the reference is to *agentes in rebus*; Paulinus of Nola, Letter 8, 3, v. 12 (Letter 32 among the letters of Augustine), where he is speaking of Licentius, who was not a soldier.

2.   This was the advice Saint Ambrose gave to ecclesiastics (*The Duties of Ministers* I, 86).

3.   Saint Ambrose also urged this (Letter 19, 7).

Saint Augustine and the Child Jesus by U. Dello Zoppo, Church of the Holy Spirit, Florence, Italy.

Part III

Last Years and Death

(Chapters 27, 6 — 31)

Humility and Trust in God

6 He also told us that he had heard that same man of blessed memory give, just before his death, a very wise and devout response which he greatly praised and commended. 7 As that venerable man was in his final illness, some faithful with the rank of honorable were standing by his bed. Seeing him about to pass from this world to God, they were saddened at the thought that the Church was to be deprived of this great bishop's administration of the divine word and sacraments. They begged him therefore with tears to ask the Lord to prolong his life. But he told them: "My life has not been such as to make me ashamed of living among you; but neither am I afraid to die, for our Lord is a good Lord."[4] 8 Our own Augustine, now an old man, admired and praised this answer with its polished and balanced phrasing. He believed that the reason why Ambrose added, "nor am I afraid to die, for our Lord is a good Lord," was to keep his hearers from thinking that he was presuming on his own irreproachable life when he said, "My life has not been such as to make me ashamed of living among you." In fact, in saying this he had in mind what human beings can know of one another; but when it came to the scrutiny of divine justice he trusted rather in the good Lord, to whom indeed he daily prayed in the Lord's Prayer, *Forgive us our debts* (Matthew 6:12).

9 In this context he often referred to what a fellow bishop and close friend of his had said at the end of his life. He had gone to visit this man as he was close to death, and the man had indicated with a gesture that his departure from the world was at hand. Augustine had responded by saying that he should live on because the Church needed him. But the

man replied: "If I never had to die, fine; but if I must some day die, why not now?"   10 Augustine admired and praised this sentiment of a God-fearing man, one who had been born and raised on a country estate but had acquired little book learning.   11 Quite different were the sentiments of the sick bishop of whom Cyprian the martyr speaks in his letter on mortality: "One of our episcopal colleagues, wearied by illness and made anxious by approaching death, prayed that he might live on. As he prayed, almost at the point of death, a tall and radiant-faced young man stood beside him, clad in such awesome glory and majesty that mortal human eyes could hardly have looked upon him, and only one about to depart from the world could see him. The young man's disdain was evident in his voice as he snorted and said: "You are afraid to suffer but unwilling to depart; what I am to do with you?"[5]

Notes

4.   Paulinus, *Life of Ambrose* 45.
5.   Saint Cyprian, *Mortality* 19.

CHAPTER 28

Revision of His Works

Vandal Invasion and Siege of Hippo

1   Not long before his death[1] he reviewed the books he had dictated and published, whether in the early days of his conversion when he was still a layman or in his years as priest and then bishop. He revised and corrected anything he found to be at odds with the Church's rule (things he had dictated or written at a time when he had less knowledge and understanding of ecclesial tradition). The result was two further volumes entitled *A Revision of My Books*.[2]

2   He complained, however, that some of the brethren had taken some of his books before he could carefully correct them, although he did correct them later on.[3] Some of his books he left incomplete because death prevented him from finishing them.[4]

3   In order to help all, whether or not they were capable of reading many books, he extracted the divine precepts and prohibitions from the two inspired Testaments, the Old and the New. He wrote a preface for the collection and made it into a single book, so that those who wished might read it and see to what extent they were obedient or disobedient to God. This work he wished to be known as the *Mirror*.[5]

4   Not long after, by permission of almighty God,[6] a vast army, equipped with varied weapons and experienced in war, came by ship from Spain across the sea and poured into Africa.[7] It was made up of savage hordes of Vandals and Alans, intermingled with Goths and men of various other nations.   5 These overran the Mauretanias[8] and reached our own provinces and districts. In their rage they displayed an utterly atrocious cruelty and laid waste to everything

with looting, slaughter, and all kinds of tortures, fire, and countless other unspeakable enormities. They had no pity on either sex or age, or even on the priests and ministers of God, or on the ornaments or furnishings or buildings of the Churches.

6   The man of God did not think and judge as others did of this savage aggression and devastation that had been and was still being inflicted by the enemy. He looked to the deeper meaning of events and foresaw chiefly the dangers and even death they brought to souls. And because, as scripture says, *He who increases knowledge increases sorrow* (Ecclesiastes 1:18) and *an understanding heart is a worm in the bones* (Proverbs 14:30; 25:20),[9] tears were more than ever his food by day and by night (Psalm 42:4). The part of his life that he endured almost at the very end was thus the bitterest and saddest of his old age.   7 For the man of God saw cities destroyed, farm buildings razed and their inhabitants either slaughtered by the enemy or put to flight and scattered, churches stripped of their priests and ministers, consecrated virgins and men vowed to continence scattered in all directions. Of the latter, some died of their tortures, others were killed with the sword, and still others fell into captivity, where they lost innocence of soul and body and even their faith in a baneful and harsh slavery to the enemy.   8 Hymns and praises of God had disappeared from the churches; in most places church buildings were put to the torch; the solemn sacrifices owed to God were no longer offered in the proper places; the divine sacraments were no longer requested or, if they were requested, no one was readily found to administer them.

9   Some people fled to the wooded hills, rocky caverns and caves, or any fortified place; others were overpowered and taken prisoner; still others, being robbed and deprived of the necessities of life, wasted away of hunger. The heads of churches and other clerics who by God's favor did not encounter the enemy or, if they did, escaped were despoiled of absolutely everything and forced in their utter need to beg, nor was it possible to supply all of them with what they

needed.   10 Of the countless Churches barely three survived — those of Carthage, Hippo,[10] and Cirta, which by
God's favor were not destroyed. These cities too have
survived, having found divine and human aid (although
after Augustine's death the city of Hippo was abandoned by
its inhabitants and burned by the enemy).[11]

11   Amid all this devastation Augustine found strength in
the saying of a wise man: "No one is great who is amazed
that wood and stone collapse and mortals die."[12]   12 In his
own great wisdom he shed copious tears every day at these
calamities. A new and intense grief was added when the
same enemy came and besieged Hippo Regius, which until
then had been left untouched because Boniface, then Count,
and an army of Gothic allies had been defending it. The
enemy enclosed and besieged it for almost fourteen months,
having blockaded even the seacoast.[13]

13   I myself, along with fellow bishops from the neighboring
districts, had taken refuge in the city and remained there
throughout the siege. Therefore we talked together very
frequently and would say, as we reflected on the fearful
judgments of God that were displayed before our eyes: *You
are just, O Lord, and your judgment is equitable* (Psalm 118:137).
In our common sorrow we groaned and wept as we prayed
to the Father of mercies and the God of all consolation (2
Corinthians 1:3) that he would deign to assist us in our trials.

Notes

1. Various dates have been suggested for the *Revisions*: 426, 427, or
428.

2. *Retractationes* (meaning "revisions") is the usual Latin title; it was
used or suggested by Augustine himself at the end of the work and in
other places where he refers to it (for example, Letter 224, 2; *The Gift of
Perseverance* 55; *The Predestination of the Saints* 7-8) and passed on by
Prosper, Cassiodorus, and Bede.

3. The reference is to the first twelve books of *The Trinity*, which
Augustine had begun in 397; these were taken and passed around before
he could correct them and finish Book 12; as a result, he decided not to
complete the work, but he subsequently yielded to the entreaties of the
brethren and completed what he had written, publishing it in about 416.
He later added three more books which appeared in 418 or 419.

4. In his catalogue Possidius mentions the *Response to Julian's Second Answer* and *Heresies*.

5. The book in question is the one known from its opening Latin words as *Speculum, Quis ignorat* (Mirror: Who does not know . . .?) to distinguish it from three other works that also have the title *Speculum* (Mirror) and are wrongly attributed to Saint Augustine. This kind of compilation was more useful in that age when many could not read or possess their own bible. Saint Cyprian had provided a similar compilation in his *Testimonies Addressed to Quirinus*. In stating the content and purpose of the work, Possidius is faithfully summarizing what Augustine says in his preface to it.

6. Possidius means that divine justice was using the barbarian invaders to punish the sins of the Africans. According to Salvian of Marseilles, who paints a very black picture of African morals, the Vandals themselves admitted that they had acted not on their own initiative but in obedience to a divine command (*Divine Governance* 7, 54). According to Procopius (*Vandal War* 1 5, 25), this was Genseric's view.

7. The barbarians invaded Africa in 428 at the summons of Count Boniface.

8. There were two provinces: Mauretania Tingitana, in the west, opposite the coast of Spain, and Mauretania Caesariensis, further east.

9. According to a Latin version that predated the Vulgate.

10. The thesis of E. C. Howard in *Journal of Roman Studies* 14 (1924) 256f., that the reference here is to Hippo Diarrhytos (modern Bizerte) and not to Hippo Regius, where Augustine lived, was refuted by Holmes V. M. Dennis, *ibid.*, 15 (1925) 263-268.

11. In all probability this happened between 432 and 435 according to Dennis (see preceding note).

12. Augustine cites this saying in almost identical words in Sermon 279, 7; see *The City of God* 2, 2; Sermon 81, 9. The "wise man" was Plotinus in *Enneads* 1, 4, 7. In any case, the thought was a commonplace, especially in the literature of consolation to sufferers: see, for example, Cicero, *Letters to Friends* 4, 5, 4 (imitated by Saint Ambrose, Letter 39, 3); Seneca, Letter 91. On the transiency of human life see the fine passage in Saint Augustine, *Expositions of the Psalms* 109, 20.

13. The siege, which is also mentioned by Victor of Vita, *History of the Persecution of the Province of Africa* 1, 3, 11, and Procopius, *Vandal War* I, 3, 3, must have begun at the end of May or the beginning of June, 430.

CHAPTER 29

Final Illness and Last Good Works

1   On one occasion he said, as we sat with him at table and were discussing these matters: "You know that during our present disaster I pray God to deliver this city from the enemies that surround it or, if he decide differently, to make his servants strong in accepting his will or at least to take me from the present world to himself."   2 He said this in part for our instruction; from that point on, therefore, we joined him in offering the same prayer for ourselves and all our fellow Christians and all who were in the city.

3   In the third month of the siege he took to his bed with a fever; it was his final illness. Nor did the Lord deprive his servant of the fruits of his prayer; for in due time he obtained what he had asked both for himself and for the city with tearful prayers.[1]   4 I know, moreover, that when as priest and as bishop he was asked to intercede for those afflicted by evil spirits he beseeched God with tears, and the demons departed from these persons.

5   Again when he lay sick in bed someone came with a sick relative and asked him to lay hands on the man in order that he might be cured.[2] Augustine answered that if he had any power in these matters he would have used it for himself first of all. The visitor replied that he had had a vision and had been told in a dream: "Go to Bishop Augustine and have him impose hands on the man, and the man will be made healthy." On hearing this, Augustine did not delay to do as he was asked, and the Lord immediately caused the sick man to leave Augustine's presence in good health.

Notes

1.   For himself Augustine asked and obtained that the Lord should not delay in calling him to his heavenly home. As for the city, Possidius seems to corroborate the account in Procopius, *Vandal War* 1, 3, 34, according to which the barbarians, seeing that the siege would be long drawn out, lifted it so that the inhabitants might depart and be saved. They then torched the city; it was not completely destroyed, however, since Augustine's library could be salvaged (see Possidius, chapter 18, 9).

2.   For the imposition of hands as a "rite of healing" see J. Coppens, *L'imposition des mains et les rites connexes dans le Nouveau Testament et dans l'Eglise ancienne* (Wetteren and Paris, 1925), 28-109.

CHAPTER 30

Advice to Bishop Honoratus
on the Conduct of the Clergy in Face of the Invaders

1   There is another incident that must by all means be recorded. While the enemies of whom I have spoken were threatening us, our holy fellow bishop, Honoratus of Thiabe,[1] wrote to Augustine, asking him whether or not bishops and clergy should leave their Churches at the arrival of the enemy. In his answer Augustine indicated what he thought was most to be feared from these destroyers of Romania.[2]   2   I have decided to include the letter[3] in this biography because it is very useful and even indispensable in deciding on the conduct of God's priests and ministers.

3   "Augustine sends greetings in the Lord to his holy[4] brother and fellow bishop Honoratus.

"I thought that by sending your Grace[5] a copy of the letter I had written to our brother and fellow bishop Quodvultdeus[6] I would be relieved of the burden you were laying on me when you asked advice on your course of action in these perilous times.   4   That letter was indeed a short one, but I believe I included everything the respondent needed to say and the inquirer to hear. I said, in fact, that on the one hand, those who wish to take refuge, if possible, in fortified places are not to be prevented and that, on the other, we are not to break the bonds by which love of Christ binds us to our ministry and to abandon the churches we are obliged to serve.   5   Here are the actual words I used in that letter: "If even a tiny portion of God's people remains in the place where we are, then, since our ministry is so indispensable that even that tiny portion must not be deprived of it, we can only say to the Lord: *Be for us the God who protects and a fortified place* (Psalm 31:3).

6   "But you have written in reply that this advice does not satisfy you, for you fear that in following it we will be acting against the command of the Lord who told us to flee from town to town; and in fact we recall his words: *When they persecute you in this town, flee to another* (Matthew 10:23).

7   "But can anyone believe the Lord meant by this that the flocks he bought with his blood are to be deprived of the ministry they need for their very life?   8   Is that what he himself was doing when as a child he fled to Egypt in the arms of his parents? Was he abandoning churches he had not even founded as yet?   9   When Paul the Apostle had himself lowered from a window in a basket and fled to avoid arrest by his enemy,[7] was he depriving the Church in that place of the ministry it needed? Was this not rather supplied by the other brethren there? In fact, the Apostle acted as he did because these others wanted to preserve for the Church the very man the persecutor was seeking.

10   "Let the ministers of Christ, then, the stewards of his word and sacrament, do as he commanded or permitted. Let them by all means flee from town to town when someone of them is being especially sought by the persecutors, provided the others who are not being specially sought out do not abandon the Church but continue to supply their fellow servants with the food (see Matthew 24:45) without which, as they well know, they cannot survive.   11   But when the danger extends to all alike, that is, to bishops and clergy and laity, those who need others may not be abandoned by those whom they need. In this case, either let everyone move to fortified positions or let those who must remain not be abandoned by those who supply their ministerial needs. Let them all alike survive or let them all alike suffer what the Father of the family wills them to suffer.

12   "If indeed they be destined to suffer, whether equally or unequally, it will become clear which of them are suffering for others. I mean those who might have fled and saved themselves from these evils but chose instead to remain and not abandon others in their need. This is the supreme proof of that love which John the Apostle urges upon us when he

says: *As Christ laid down his life for us, so we ought to lay down our lives for the brethren* (1 John 3:16).   13 Those who flee or, being unable to flee because prevented by their own interests, are caught and made to suffer, evidently suffer in their own behalf and not in behalf of others. Those on the other hand who suffer because they were unwilling to abandon the brethren who needed them for their salvation as Christians undoubtedly lay down their lives for their brothers and sisters.

14   "We have heard one bishop say: 'If the Lord has bidden us to flee amid persecutions that might have yielded the fruit of martyrdom, how much more should we flee the barren sufferings inflicted by an invading barbarian foe?' The saying is valid and can be accepted, but only by those not bound by the duties of an ecclesiastical office.   15 One who could flee a slaughtering enemy but does not do so lest he abandon the ministry of Christ without which men and women cannot become and live as Christians yields greater fruits of love than one who flees for his own sake rather than for the sake of the brethren, but then is captured and, refusing to deny Christ, suffers martyrdom.

16   "What, then, were you thinking of when you wrote in your earlier letter: 'I do not see what good we will do either for ourselves or for our people if we must remain in our churches only to see men slain, women raped, and churches burned before our eyes, and to die ourselves under torture as they seek from us what we do not have.'   17 God, after all, is powerful enough to hear the prayers of his family and avert the diasters they fear! Furthermore, all these disasters, which are uncertain, do not not authorize what is certainly an abandonment of a ministry without which the people will certainly suffer loss, not in the affairs of the present life but in those of that other life that is to be sought with incomparably greater diligence and anxiety.   18 For if the evils which we fear may occur where we live were inevitable, all those people for whose sake we must remain would have already fled, thus freeing us of the obligation to remain. For no one will claim that ministers must remain where there is no one

left who needs their services.   19 Thus some holy bishops fled Spain[8] when some of their people had fled, others had been killed, still others had died in the siege, and the remainder had been taken prisoner and dispersed. Many more bishops, however, remained in the midst of these dangers, because the people for whose sake they were remaining had themselves stayed. Some indeed abandoned their people, but this, I am saying, is what they should not have done. These individuals were not so instructed by divine authority, but were misled by human error or yielded to human fear.

20 "Why do they think they must obey without qualification the command to flee from town to town, but do not fear becoming hirelings who *see the wolf coming and run off because they are not concerned about the sheep* (John 10:12)? Both are true sayings of the Lord: the one allowing or commanding flight, the other rebuking and condemning it. Why do they not try to interpret them as compatible with one another, as in fact they are?   21 But they will not discover this compatibility unless they pay heed to the interpretation I gave above: that when persecution is imminent, we ministers of Christ are to flee from the places in which we are living, provided that there are none of Christ's followers there for us to serve or, if there are, others who do not have the same reason for fleeing can provide the needed ministries.

22 "Thus the Apostle, as I said above, was lowered in a basket and fled when he individually was being sought by the persecutor, while others not in similar straits could see to it that the Church was not — God forbid! — deprived of the ministry. So, too, holy Athanasius, bishop of Alexandria, fled when Emperor Constantius was trying to lay hands on him specifically;[9] but the other ministers did not abandon the Catholic people who remained in Alexandria.   23 But when the people remain and the ministers flee and leave them with no one to minister to them, can the behavior of the latter be described as anything but a despicable flight of hirelings who have no interest in the sheep? Then the wolf will come: not some human being, but the devil, who often

persuades the faithful to apostatize when they lack the daily ministry of the Lord's body.[10] Then the weak brother for whom Christ died will perish, not through your knowledge but through ignorance.[11]

24 "As for those who have correct ideas on this point but nonetheless are overcome by fear, why do they not rather struggle courageously against their fear, with the help of a merciful God, lest they suffer incomparably greater evils that are far more to be feared?   25 That is the course of action human beings follow when the love of God burns strong in them, and not the smoky passions of the world. For love says: *Who is weak, and I am not also weak? Who is scandalized, and I do not burn with indignation?* (2 Corinthians 11:29). But love has its origin in God. Let us pray, therefore, that he who commands love may also bestow it.[12] And let this love make us fear more the sword of spiritual wickedness (see Ephesians 6:12) that kills the hearts of Christ's sheep than the sword of iron that kills their bodies; in body, after all, they must someday suffer one or other kind of death. 26 Yes, let us fear more that the interior sense be perverted and lose the purity of faith than that women may be raped in the flesh; for chastity is not destroyed by violence as long as it is preserved in intention; in fact, even bodily chastity is not destroyed when the will of the sufferer does not deliberately use the flesh shamefully but only endures the action of another without giving consent to it.[13]   27 Let us fear rather that the living stones may be deprived of life if we abandon them, than that the stones and wood of earthly buildings may be burned in our presence. Let us fear rather that the members of Christ's body may be slain through deprivation of their spiritual food than that the members of our own bodies may be overwhelmed by the attack of the enemy and subjected to torture.   28 I do not mean that all these sufferings should not be avoided if possible; but if they cannot be avoided without our failing in our duty, then they must be endured. Or will someone maintain that a minister is not wicked who refuses his ministry, which is always necessary for religion, and does so at the very time when it is most needed?

29 "Do we not reflect that when these dangers become most pressing and flight is impossible, a great throng of people of both sexes and all ages usually flocks to the Church, some of them asking for baptism, others for reconciliation, others still for a penance to be performed,[14] and all of them for strength and for the consecration and distribution of the sacraments?   **30** If ministers are then lacking, what ruin awaits those who leave this world still not reborn[15] or still bound by their sins! What grief for their brothers and sisters in the faith who will not enjoy their company in the repose of eternal life! What lamentations on all sides and, in some cases, what blasphemies at the absence of ministries and ministers!

31 "See what effects the fear of temporal evils produces and what terrible evils it causes in eternity! If, however, ministers are present, they help everyone according to the strength the Lord gives them: some are baptized, others are reconciled, no one is deprived of communion in the Lord's body, all are strengthened, built up, and encouraged to pray to God who has power to ward off all the evils they fear. All are prepared for whatever comes, so that if this cup may not pass from them, his will may be done (see Matthew 26:42) who cannot will anything that is evil.

32 "You surely see now what you said you did not see, that is, how greatly Christian peoples benefit if in the present calamities they have Christ's ministers present among them. You see, too, what great harm these ministers do by their absence as they seek their own interests and not those of Jesus Christ (Philippians 2:21).

"Such men do not have that virtue[16] of which it is said: *It does not seek its own interests* (1 Corinthians 13:5), nor do they imitate him who said: *Seeking not my own advantage but the advantage of the many, that they may be saved* (1 Corinthians 10:33).   **33** He would not have fled the snares of the persecuting prince,[17] were he not saving himself for the sake of others who needed him. That is why he says: *I am pulled in two directions: I desire to depart and be with Christ, for that is far better; but I must remain in the flesh for your sake* (Philippians 1:23).

34 "At this point someone may say that Christ's ministers ought to flee when such disasters are imminent, in order that they may survive to be of use to the Church in more tranquil times. Some do so, and they act rightly, provided others are available who will carry on the ministry of the Church and not let it be completely abandoned. Athanasius, for example, whom I mentioned earlier, acted in this way, and the Catholic faith, which he defended by word and by love against the Arian heretics, is aware how much the Church needed him and how much it profited from his remaining alive.   35 But by no means should a minister act in this way when everyone is in danger and it is to be feared that his conduct will be attributed more to fear of death than to a desire to provide for others; in other words, when the harm done by the example of his flight outweighs any advantage to be gained by his dutifully remaining alive.   36 Finally, when holy David did not risk the perils of battle lest, as it is put there, *the lamp of Israel be quenched* (2 Samuel 21:17), he was yielding to the pleas of his followers and not taking the decision upon himself. For if it had been his own spontaneous decision, many would have imitated him out of cowardice, thinking that he was acting not from concern for the good of others but simply from fear of the danger to himself.

37 "Another question arises that is not to be taken lightly. If the advantage of others is not simply to be left out of account and if, therefore, when a disaster is imminent, some ministers may flee precisely in order to serve the needs of those who survive the calamity, what is to be done when there is reason to believe that all will perish if some do not flee? What if the persecutors seek out only the ministers of the Church?

38 "What are we to say? That the Church's ministers should flee and abandon it lest it be even more abandoned if they die! Moreover, if the laity are not being sought for execution, surely they can somehow manage to hide their bishops and clerics with the help of him who has all things under his control and whose wonderful might can save even those who do not flee.

39 "We ask, nonetheless, what we ought to do so as not to

seem to tempt the Lord by always looking for miracles from on high.

"A storm of persecution that endangers laity and clergy alike cannot be compared to a storm that endangers merchants and sailors alike aboard a ship. Far be it from us to set such little value on this ship of ours as to say that its sailors, and especially its pilot, should abandon it in moments of danger, even though they might save themselves by taking to a small boat or by swimming.

40 "Why so? Because the death we fear for others who may die as a result of our desertion is not temporal death, which must come to them someday in any case, but eternal death, which may come to them if care is not taken but can be avoided if care is taken.   41 Why, then, do we think that in the shared dangers of this life, as, for example, when an enemy invades, all the clergy will die but not all the laity and that all will not end together this life during which the clergy are required? Or why do we not hope that just as some of the laity will survive, so also will some of the clergy and be able to supply them with the ministry they need?

42 "If only the disagreement among God's ministers were about which of them are to remain lest the Church be abandoned by the flight of all, and which of them are to flee lest the Church be abandoned by the death of all! That is the kind of disagreement that arises when both sides are inspired by love and are pleasing to Love.[18]

43 "If such a disagreement cannot be otherwise settled, then, in my opinion, the choice of who is to stay and who to flee will have to be made by drawing lots. For those who say they ought to flee will seem either fearful, as though unable to endure the imminent disaster, or arrogant, as though believing themselves more necessary to the Church and therefore to be rescued.   44 Furthermore, the best will probably choose to lay down their lives for the brethren, while those whose lives are less useful because they have less ability to counsel and govern will be saved by flight. But the latter, if they have the Christian mind, will oppose those whom they see preferring death to flight when in fact they

have a duty rather to continue living.   45 Therefore, as it is written, *the lot puts an end to disputes and decides between powerful contenders* (Proverbs 18:18). In this kind of doubt God is a better judge than human beings, whether he deign to call the better to the palm of martyrdom while sparing the weak or to strengthen the weak for suffering and to take them from the present life since their lives here cannot be as useful to the Church as the lives of the others. Drawing lots is indeed an unusual procedure, but if it is used who will dare find it blameworthy? Who but the ignorant or the malicious will not praise it as it deserves?

46   "If this procedure be found unacceptable because there is no precedent for it, then let no one by fleeing deprive the Church of the ministry that is all the more necessary and owing to it in such times of danger. Let no one give preference to himself and say that because he has this or that excellent quality he deserves to live and therefore to flee. Anyone who thinks in this way is overly pleased with himself; anyone who talks in this way is displeasing to everyone else.[19]

47   "In the view of some, bishops and clerics who do not flee such dangers but remain in them mislead their congregations because when the latter see their leaders remaining they too remain.   48 But this charge and the malice that inspires it can easily be avoided by addressing the people and telling them: 'Do not be misled by our failure to flee. We are remaining not for our own sake but for yours, so as not to deprive you of any ministry which we know you need for your salvation in Christ. Therefore, if you flee, you will at the same time release us from the obligation that keeps us here.'   49 I think that this kind of thing has to be said when it seems really more advisable to take refuge in safer locations. After it has been said, all or some may say: 'We are in the power of him whose anger none can flee no matter where they go and whose mercy can be found by all, wherever they are, even if they refuse to go elsewhere because they are prevented by definite obligations or are

unwilling to hunt out an unsure refuge and to exchange dangers rather than end them.' Such people are certainly not to be abandoned by Christ's ministers. If, on the other hand, the people heed the words of their leaders and decide to flee, then those who would have remained for their sake need no longer remain, since those for whose sake they would have been obliged to remain have themselves departed.

50   "Those, then, whose flight does not deprive the Church of the ministry it needs act in accordance with the command or permission of the Lord. Those, on the other hand, whose flight deprives Christ's flock of the food for its spiritual life are hirelings who see the wolf coming and flee because they care nothing for the sheep (John 10:12).

51   "Dear brother, you have asked me for guidance; I have told you what I think right and, in any case, have answered with unfeigned love; if you find better counsel, I make no claim to tell you what you ought to think. Be that as it may, our best course in the present dangers is to pray to the Lord our God to have mercy on us. It is by his gift that various prudent and holy men have found the desire and strength not to abandon their churches, and have persevered in their firm resolve in the face of detractors."

Notes

1.   Or Tiabena (according to Augustine, Letter 73, 1), a small town located probably between Thagaste and Hippo.

2.   *Romania,* a name modelled on *Gallia, Graecia, Brittania,* and others, occurs first in Orosius, *History against the Pagans* 3, 20, 11; 7, 43, 5.

3.   The letter is number 228 in the collection of Augustine's letters. D. De Bruyne (*Revue benedictine* 42 [1930] 300) thinks that Possidius himself published this letter, which was probably Augustine's final composition; once the siege began, Augustine no longer had the leisure to publish his letters, as he had done previously. The fortunes of this particular letter in the manuscript tradition seems to support De Bruyne's view, which would also explain why Possidius includes so lengthy a document: he would have found it in the library of the Church of Hippo and realized that it would otherwise not come to the attention of readers.

4.   See above, note 1 of Chapter 4.

5.   Literally, "Your Charity" (*Caritas tua*).

6.   The letter has not survived. We do not know who this Quodvultdeus was; it was certainly not the better known Quodvultdeus, Bishop of Carthage, since he became bishop only in 437. Several other bishops contemporary with Augustine bore this same name.

7.   The reference is to Aretas, ethnarch of Damacus; see 2 Corinthians 11:32-33.

8.   In 410, when Alaric was capturing Rome, barbarian tribes — Sueves, Vandals, Alans — entered the Iberian peninsula, laying it waste and dividing up the territory among them; a short time later, the Visigoths settled there under Athaulf, who was succeeded in 415 by Wallia.

9.   Athanasius twice fled to safety from persecution by Constantius, in 339 and 356; Augustine seems to be referring to the second episode.

10.   In eucharistic communion; see below, section 30 of this chapter.

11.   As in the case to which Saint Paul refers in his rebuke, 1 Corinthians 8:11.

12.   A thought familiar to Saint Augustine, especially in the Pelagian controversy; see *Confessions* 10, 29, 40: "Give me the grace to do as you command, and command me to do what you will." Latin: "Da quod iubes, et iube quod vis."

13.   Same thought elsewhere in Augustine: *The City of God* I, 16; *Against Julian* 4, 14; *Letter* 3, 9.

14.   The public penance required for more serious sins had to be requested by the guilty party. The time for its performance was not specified, and since such penance was not permitted more than once, many individuals put it off to the end of their lives (see Ambrose's objections to this thinking in his *Penance* 2, 98-100). Reconciliation, that is, readmission to full communion with the Church, was granted after completion of the penance or even before it when there was danger of death; it is this latter situation that Augustine has in mind here.

15.   Through baptism.

16.   The virtue of charity.

17.   Aretas (see note 9).

18.   That is, to God, of whom it is said: *God is love* (1 John 4:16).

19.   Same play on words in Ambrose, *Virginity* 1, 28, who is cited by Augustine in his *Christian Instruction* 4, 50.

Last Days of Augustine by Mattäus Günther, 1755, Indersdorf, West Germany.

Death of Augustine by Ottaviano Nelli (1375-1444/50), Church of Saint Augustine, Gubbio, Italy.

CHAPTER 31

Last Days and Death
A Legacy of Holy Deeds and Example
Conclusion

1   God granted this holy man a long life for the benefit and prosperity of his holy Church (he lived seventy-six years, almost forty of them as a cleric and bishop).[1] In intimate conversations with us he used to say that after receiving baptism even exemplary Christians and bishops should not depart from this life without having repented worthily and adequately.   2 That is precisely what he himself did in his final illness; he had the very few Davidic psalms on repentance[2] written out and the sheets attached to the wall opposite his bed; then, while he lay ill, he looked at them, read them, and wept continually and copiously.

3   In order that his recollection might not be broken, about ten days before departing from the body he asked us who were present not to let anyone in to see him except when the doctors came to examine him or his meals were brought to him. His wish was carefully respected, and he spent the entire time in prayer.

4   Right down to his final illness he preached the word of God in the church uninterruptedly, zealously, and courageously, and with soundness of mind and judgment.   5 Then, with all his bodily members still intact and with sight and hearing undiminished, as we stood by watching and praying, he fell asleep with his fathers (as scripture says)[3] in a good old age.[4] A sacrifice[5] was offered to God in our presence to commend his bodily death,[6] and then he was buried.

6   He did not make a will because as a poor man of God he had nothing to leave. He always intended that the library of

the church and all the books in it should be carefully preserved for posterity. Any money or ornaments the church might have were entrusted to the care of the priest who was in charge of the church house while he himself was superior.[7]

7   Neither in life nor in death did he treat his relatives, whether in monastic life[8] or outside it, as others usually treat theirs. While he was still alive, he gave to them, if need be, as he did to others, not to make them rich but to keep them from want or at least to make them less needy.

8   His legacy to the Church was a very numerous clergy and monasteries filled with men and women vowed to continence under the guidance of their superiors, as well as libraries containing his own books and discourses and those of other holy men.[9] From these, God be thanked, we can know his quality and importance as a churchman; in them he will always be alive for the faithful. So too, one of the secular poets dictated the following epitaph for the tomb which he ordered built for himself by a public road:[10] "Traveller, would you know how a poet, dead, lives on? When you read, I speak, and your voice is mine."[11]

9   From the writings of this priest, so pleasing and dear to God, it is clear, as far as the light of truth allows humans to see, that he led a life of uprightness and integrity in the faith, hope, and love of the Catholic Church. This is certainly acknowledged by those who read his writings on the things of God. I believe, however, that they profited even more who were able to hear him speaking in church and see him there present, especially if they were familiar with his manner of life among his fellow human beings.   10 Not only was he a teacher learned in the kingdom of heaven, who brings forth things new and old from his storeroom (Matthew 13:52), and one of those merchants who on finding a precious pearl sells what he has and buys it (Matthew 13:45-46). He was also one of those regarding whom it was written: *So speak and so act* (James 2:12), and of whom the Savior says: *He who does these things and teaches them to others will be called great in the kingdom of heaven* (Matthew 5:19).

11   I earnestly beseech you, my readers, that in your charity you would join me in thanking almighty God and blessing the Lord who has given me understanding (Psalm 16:7) and made me willing and able to bring these matters to the knowledge of all both here and elsewhere, both now and in the future. I ask you also to pray for me that after having by God's gift lived with this man for almost forty years, without bitterness or dissension and in sweet familiarity, I may emulate and imitate him in the present world and enjoy the promises of almighty God with him in the world to come.

Notes

1.   From the early months of 391, when he was ordained a priest.

2.   In the liturgy as we know it today Psalms 6, 32, 38, 51, 102, 130, and 143 (Vulgate: 6, 31, 37, 50, 101, 129, and 142) are known as the "penitential psalms." It is to these that Possidius is apparently referring when he speaks of "the very few Davidic psalms on repentance."

3.   See 1 Kings 2:10: *Then David slept with his fathers,* and 2 Chronicles 29:28: *Then he [David] died in a good old age.*

4.   On 28 August 430.

5.   The Mass, according to a traditional practice already attested by Saint Cyprian (Letter 1, 2), Saint Ambrose, *On the Death of His Brother Satyrus* 1, 80; On the Death of Valentinian 56, 78; Letter 39, 4; Paulinus (*The Life of Ambrose* 48), and Saint Augustine himself (*Confessions* 9, 12, 29 and 32; *Handbook* 110; *The Care To Be Taken of the Dead* 22; Sermons 159, 1; 172, 2; *Homilies on the Gospel of John* 84, 1; *Virginity* 46). And see J. A. Jungmann, *The Mass of the Roman Rite: Its Origins and Development (Missarum Solemnia,* trans. F. A. Brunner, 1) (New York, 1951), page 170.

6.   *Depositio* often means burial, which Christians understood as a simple entrusting of the body to the earth, which would give it up again at the resurrection; but "depositio" can also mean death, and certainly does so here.

7.   See Chapter 24, 1.

8.   In Sermon 365, 3 Augustine speaks of a nephew, Patricius, as being a cleric in his monastery.

9.   The adjective "holy" indicates here, as often elsewhere, ecclesiastics or, perhaps, simply "good Christians." "Libraries" in the plural: monasteries of women also had libraries (see Letter 311, 13).

10.   For this meaning of *agger publicus* see *Thesaurus Linguae Latinae* I, 1309 (where, however, this passage is not cited).

11.   Verse of an unknown pagan poet in the *Anthologia Latina,* no. 721. The thought was in all probability a commonplace.

Augustine in his study by Sandro Botticelli (1445-1510), Uffizi Gallery, Florence, Italy.

English Titles of the Works of Augustine

Adulterous Marriages (De adulterinis conjugiis)
The Advantage of Believing (De utilitate credendi)
The Advantage of Fasting (De utilitate ieiunandi)
Against Lying (Contra mendacium)
Agreement among the Evangelists (De consensu evangelistarum)
Answer to Adimantus, a Disciple of Mani (Contra Adimantum Manichaei discipulum)
Answer to an Arian Sermon (Contra sermonem Arianorum)
Answer to Centurius' Report on the Donatists (Contra quod attulit Centurius a Donatistis) *Lost*
Answer to Cresconius (Contra Cresconium)
Answer to the Donatist Party (Contra partem Donati) *Lost*
Answer to an Enemy of the Law and the Prophets (Contra adversarium Legis et Prophetarum)
Answer to Faustus, a Manichean (Contra Faustum Manichaeum)
Answer to Felix, a Manichean (Contra Felicem Manichaeum)
Answer to Fortunatus, a Manichean (Contra Fortunatum Manichaeum)
Answer to Gaudentius, a Donatist Bishop (Contra Gaudentium Donatistarum episcopum)
Answer to Hilary (Contra Hilarium) *Lost*
Answer to the Jews (Adversus Judaeos)
Answer to Julian (Contra Julianum)
Answer to the Letter of Donatus the Heretic (Contra epistulam Donati heretici) *Lost*
Answer to the Letter of Mani Known as "The Foundation" (Contra epistulam Manichaei quam vocant "Fundamenti")
Answer to Maximinus the Arian(Contra Maximinum Arianum)
Answer to the Letter of Parmenian (Contra epistulam Parmeniani)
Answer to the Questions of Januarius (Ad inquisitiones Ianuarii - Letters 54-55)
Answer to Secundinus (Contra Secundinum)
Answer to the Skeptics (Contra Academicos)
Answer to Two Letters of the Pelagians (Contra dua epistulas Pelagianorum)
Answer to an Unidentified Donatist (Contra nescio quem Donatistam) *Lost*
Answer to the Writings of Petilian (Contra litteras Petiliani)

Arithmetic (De arithmetica) *Lost*
Baptism (De baptismo)
The Beautiful and the Fitting (De pulchro et apto) *Lost*
The Care to be Taken of the Dead (De cura pro mortuis gerenda)
The Catholic Way of Life and the Manichean Way of Life (De moribus Ecclesiae catholicae et de moribus Manichaeorum)
The Chastisement of the Donatists (De correctione Donatistarum - Letter 185)
Christian Instruction (De doctrina christiana)
The Christian Combat (De agone christiano)
The City of God (De civitate Dei)
Commentary on the Letter to the Galatians (Epistulae ad Galatas expositio)
Commentary on the Letter of James to the Twelve Tribes (Expositio epistulae Iacobi ad duodecim tribus) *Lost*
Commentary on Some Statements in the Letter to the Romans (Expositio quarundam propositionum ex epistula ad Romanos)
Continence (De continentia)
Correction and Grace (De correptione et gratia)
Confessions (Confessiones)
Debate with Maximinus (Collatio cum Maximino)
The Deeds of Pelagius (De gestis Pelagii)
The Destruction of the City of Rome (De excidio urbis Romae)
Dialectic (De dialectica)
The Divination of Demons (De divinatione daemonum)
Eight Questions of Dulcitius (De VIII Dulcitii quaestionibus)
Eight Questions on the Old Testament (De octo quaestionibus ex Vetere Testamento)
The Excellence of Marriage (De bono conjugali)
The Excellence of Widowhood (De bono viduitatis)
Expositions of the Psalms (Enarrationes in psalmos)
Faith and the Creed (De fide et symbolo)
Faith and Works (De fide et operibus)
Faith, Hope, and Charity [See: Handbook]
Faith in the Unseen (De fide rerum invisibilium)
Free Will (De libero arbitrio)
Geometry (De geometria) *Lost*
The Gift of Perseverance (De dono perseverantiae)
Grace and Free Will (De gratia et libero arbitrio)
The Grace of Christ and Original Sin (De gratia Christi et de peccato originali)

The Grace of the New Testament, to Honoratus (De gratia testamenti novi ad Honoratum - Letter 140)

Grammar (De grammatica)

Handbook for Lawrence, or: Faith, Hope, and Charity (Enchiridion ad Laurentium, seu de fide, spe, et caritate)

The Happy Life (De beata vita)

Heresies (De haeresibus)

Holy Virginity (De sancta virginitate)

Homilies on the Gospel of John (In Joannis evangelium tractatus)

Homilies on the First Letter of John (In Joannis epistulam ad Parthos tractatus)

The Immortality of the Soul (De immortalitate animae)

The Instruction of Beginners (De catechizandis rudibus)

A Letter to Catholics on the Donatist Sect, or: The Unity of the Church (Epistula ad Catholicos de secta Donatistarum, seu De unitate Ecclesiae)

Letters (Epistulae)

The Literal Meaning of Genesis (De Genesi ad litteram)

The Lord's Sermon on the Mount (De sermone Domini in monte)

Lying (De mendacio)

The Magnitude of the Soul (De quantitate animae)

The Manichean Way of Life [See: The Catholic Way . . .]

Marriage and Desire (De nuptiis et concupiscentia)

The Merits and Forgiveness of Sins and the Baptism of Infants (De peccatorum meritis et remissione et de baptismo parvulorum)

Mirror: "Who Does not Know?" (Speculum: Quis ignorat)

Miscellany of Eighty-three Questions (De diversis quaestionibus LXXXIII)

Miscellany of Questions in Response to Simplician (De diversis quaestionibus ad Simplicianum)

Music (De musica)

Nature and Grace (De natura et gratia)

The Nature and Origin of the Soul (De natura et originae animae)

The Nature of the Good (De natura boni)

Notes on Job (Adnotationes in Iob)

Observations on the Heptateuch (Locutiones in Heptateuchum)

On Genesis: A Refutation of the Manicheans (De genesis contra Manichaeos)

On the Maximianists, in Response to the Donatists (De Maximianistis contra Donatistas) *Lost*

The One Baptism, in Answer to Petilian (De unico baptismo contra Petilianum)

Order (De ordine)

Patience (De patientia)

The Perfection of Human Righteousness (De perfection iustitiae humanae)

Philosophy (De philosophia) *Lost*

Prayer of Saint Augustine for His Book on the Trinity (Oratio S. Augustini in librum de Trinitate)

The Predestination of the Saints (De praedestinatione sanctorum)

The Presence of God, to Dardanus (De praesentia Dei ad Dardanum - Letter 187)

Proceedings with Emeritus (De actis cum Emerito)

Proceedings with Felix the Manichean (De actis cum Felice Manichaeo)

Proofs and Testimonies against the Donatists (Probationum et testimoniorum contra Donatistas liber unus) *Lost*

Psalm against the Donatist Party (Psalmus contra partem Donati)

Questions on the Gospels (Quaestiones evangeliorum)

Questions on the Heptateuch (Quaestiones in Heptateuchum)

Revisions (Retractationes)

Rhetoric (De rhetorica)

Rule (Regula)

Sermon on the Cataclysm (Sermo de cataclysmo)

Sermon on Christian Discipline (Sermo de disciplina christiana)

Sermon to Catechumens on the Creed (Sermo ad catechumenos de symbolo)

Sermon to the People of the Church of Caesarea (Sermo ad Caesariensis ecclesiae populum)

Sermons (Sermones)

Seventeen Questions on Matthew (Quaestiones XVII in Matthaeum)

Six Questions Against Pagans (Quaestiones expositae contra paganos numero sex - Letter 102)

Soliloquies (Soliloquia)

The Spirit and the Letter (De spiritu et littera)

The Statement of James (De sententia Iacobi - Letter 167)

Summary of the Conference with the Donatists (Breviculus Collationis cum Donatistis)

The Teacher (De magistro)

The Trinity (De Trinitate)

True Religion (De vera religione)

The Two Souls (De duabus animis)

To the Donatists after the Conference (Ad Donatistas post collationem)

To Emeritus, a Donatist Bishop, after the Conference (Ad Emeritum episcopus Donatistarum post collationem) *Lost*

To Orosius in Refutation of the Priscilianists and Origenists (Ad Orosium contra Priscilianistas et Origenistas)

Unfinished Commentary on the Letter to the Romans (Epistulae ad Romanos inchoata expositio)

Unfinished Literal Commentary on Genesis (De Genesi ad litteram imperfectus liber)

Unfinished Work in Answer to Julian (Opus imperfectum contra Julianum)

Unfinished Work in Refutation of Julian's Second Answer (Contra secundam Iuliani responsionem imperfectum opus)

The Unity of the Church [See: A Letter to Catholics on the Donatist Sect]

Verses on Saint Nabor (Versus de S. Nabore)

Verses Written on the Table (Versus in mensa)

The Vision of God (De videndo Deo - Letter 147)

The Work of Monks (De opere monachorum)

INDEX

Numbers in parentheses are note numbers

Index of Scripture References

Old Testament

New Testament